DRAMA CLASSICS

The Drama Classics series aims to offer the world's greatest plays in affordable paperback editions for students, actors and theatregoers. The hallmarks of the series are accessible introductions, uncluttered texts and an overall theatrical perspective.

Given that readers may be encountering a particular play for the first time, the introduction seeks to fill in the theatrical/historical background and to outline the chief themes rather than concentrate on interpretational and textual analysis. Similarly the play-texts themselves are free of footnotes and other interpolations: instead there is an end-glossary of 'difficult' words and phrases.

The texts of the English-language plays in the series have been prepared taking full account of all existing scholarship. The foreign-language plays have been newly translated into a modern English that is both actable and accurate: many of the translators regularly have their work staged professionally.

Edited until his early death by Kenneth McLeish, the Drama Classics series continues with his aim of providing a first-class library of dramatic literature representing the best of world theatre.

Associate editors:
Professor Trevor
Dr. Colin C
School of Arts
University of

DRAMA CLASSICS *the first hundred*

*The publishers welcome
suggestions for further
titles*

DRAMA CLASSICS

THE LADY
FROM THE SEA

by
Henrik Ibsen

Translated and introduced by
Kenneth McLeish

NICK HERN BOOKS
London
www.nickhernbooks.co.uk

A Drama Classic

The Lady from the Sea first published in Great Britain
in this translation as a paperback original in 2001
by Nick Hern Books Limited, 14 Larden Road, London W3 7ST

Copyright in the Introduction © 2001 by Nick Hern Books Ltd

Copyright in this translation from Norwegian © 2001
by the Estate of the late Kenneth McLeish

Kenneth McLeish died in 1997. The text has been edited, and
the introduction completed, by Stephen Mulrine

Typeset by Country Setting, Kingsdown, Kent CT14 8ES
Printed by Bath Press, Avon

A CIP catalogue record for this book is available from
the British Library

ISBN 1 85459 493 1

Introduction

Henrik Ibsen (1828-1906)

Henrik Ibsen was born on 20 March, 1828 in Skien, a small town to the south of Kristiania (now Oslo), the capital city of Norway, into a prosperous middle-class family. His mother, Marichen, took a lively interest in the arts, and Ibsen was introduced to the theatre at an early age. When he was six, however, his father's business failed, and Ibsen's childhood was spent in relative poverty, until he was forced to leave school and find employment as an apprentice pharmacist in Grimstad. In 1846, an affair with a housemaid ten years older than him produced an illegitimate son, whose upbringing Ibsen was compelled to pay for until the boy was in his teens, though he saw nothing of him. Ibsen's family relationships in general were not happy, and after the age of twenty-two, he never saw either of his parents again, and kept in touch with them only through his sister Hedvig's letters.

While still working as a pharmacist, Ibsen was studying for university, in pursuit of a vague ambition to become a doctor. He failed the entrance examination, however, and at the age of twenty, launched his literary career with the publication in 1850 of a verse play, *Catiline*, which sold a mere fifty copies, having already been rejected by the

Danish Theatre in Kristiania. Drama in Norwegian was virtually non-existent at this time, and the low status of the language reflected Norway's own position, as a province of Denmark, for most of the preceding five centuries. Kristiania, the capital, was one of Europe's smallest, with fewer than 30,000 inhabitants, and communications were primitive.

However, change, as far as the theatre was concerned, was already under way, and Ibsen and his younger contemporary Bjørnson were among the prime movers. Another was the internationally famous violinist, Ole Bull, who founded a Norwegian-language theatre in his home town of Bergen, and invited Ibsen to become its first resident dramatist in 1851, with a commitment to write one play each year, to be premièred on January 2nd, the anniversary of the theatre's founding.

During his time at Bergen, Ibsen wrote five plays, mainly historical in content: *St. John's Night*, a comedy which he later disowned, loosely based on *A Midsummer Night's Dream*; *The Warrior's Barrow*, a reworking of a one-act verse play first staged in Kristiania; *Lady Inger of Østråt*, a five-act drama set in 16th-century Trondheim, on the theme of Norwegian independence; *The Feast at Solhaug*, which went on to be commercially published; and a romantic drama, *Olaf Liljekrans*, to complete his contractual obligations in Bergen.

Ibsen had meanwhile met his future wife, Suzannah Thoresen, and the offer of a post as artistic director of the newly-created Norwegian Theatre in Kristiania must have been very welcome. Ibsen took up his post in September 1857, and not the least of his responsibilities was to compete for audiences with the long-established Danish Theatre in Kristiania. A successful first season was accordingly crucial, and his own new play, *The Vikings at Helgeland*, set in 10th-century Norway, and based on material drawn from the Norse sagas, was an important contribution. By 1861, however, the Danish Theatre was clearly winning the battle, in part by extending its Norwegian repertoire, and Ibsen's theatre was forced to close, in the summer of 1862.

Now unemployed, Ibsen successfully applied for a government grant to collect folk-tales in the Norwegian hinterland. During this period he also wrote *Love's Comedy*, a verse play on the theme of modern marriage, and a five-act historical drama, *The Pretenders*, premièred at the Kristiania Danish Theatre, now thoroughly Norwegian, in January 1864, under Ibsen's own direction. A few months later, financed by another government grant, Ibsen left Norway for Copenhagen on 2 April, 1864, beginning a journey that would take him on to Rome, and international recognition.

Brand, the first fruit of Ibsen's self-imposed exile, sees him abandoning historical themes, and drawing on his own experience more directly, basing his uncompromising hero on a fanatical priest who had led a religious revival in Ibsen's home town of Skien in the 1850s. Like all of Ibsen's plays, *Brand* was published before it was staged, in March 1866, and received its first full performance almost twenty years later, in 1885 at the Nya Theatre in Stockholm, though it seems clear that like *Peer Gynt*, his next play, *Brand* was intended to be read, rather than acted.

Ibsen wrote *Peer Gynt* at Rome, Ischia and Sorrento, through the summer of 1867, using material from Asbjørnsen's recently-published *Norwegian Folk-Tales*, as well as the darker corners of his own life, but the end result is regarded as containing some of his finest dramatic writing, with the irrepressible Peer at the other end of the moral spectrum from Brand, a typical example of Ibsen's fondness for opposites or antitheses in his dramatic work.

The following spring, Ibsen left Rome for Berchtesgaden in the Bavarian Alps, to work on a new play, *The League of Youth*, which was premièred at the Kristiania Theatre in October 1869, and attracted some hostility for its satirical portrayal of contemporary politicians. A few weeks later, Ibsen travelled to Egypt, to represent his country at the official opening of the Suez Canal.

On his return, Ibsen began work on what he regarded as his greatest achievement, the mammoth ten-act *Emperor and Galilean*, dramatising the conflict between Christianity and paganism, through the life of Julian the Apostate. Published in Copenhagen in October 1873, to critical acclaim, the play nonetheless had to wait over a century before it was staged in full, an eight-hour marathon in Oslo in 1987.

By this time, Ibsen's fame had brought him tempting offers to return to Norway, as well as recognition at the highest level in the form of a knighthood, of the Order of St Olaf. However, apart from a brief sojourn in Kristiania in the summer of 1874, he remained in Germany, moving from Dresden to Munich the following year, to commence writing *The Pillars of Society*, completed in 1877, the first in a series of 'social problem' plays, although its large cast requirements make it nowadays something of a theatrical rarity. By contrast, his next play, *A Doll's House*, has seldom been absent from the stage since its Copenhagen première in December 1879, and the challenge it offers to male hypocrisy and so-called 'family values' has ensured its continuing popularity.

In Ibsen's characteristic manner, *Ghosts* in effect reverses the situation of *A Doll's House*, showing the tragic consequences of a wife's failure to break free from a disastrous marriage. Its exposure of taboo subjects like venereal disease, however, still retains the power to shock, and it was at first rejected by all Ibsen's preferred theatres. After publication, almost two years elapsed before *Ghosts* was staged in Scandinavia, and the world première in fact took place in Chicago, in May 1882.

Ibsen was angered by his countrymen's reception of *Ghosts*, and *An Enemy of the People*, with its ill-concealed attack on the Norwegian establishment, is to an extent a vehicle for that anger, as well as for Ibsen's sceptical views on democracy. The play thus offended liberals and conservatives alike, but not enough to impede its staging, and it was premièred in Kristiania in January 1883, to mixed reviews.

The initial reaction to *The Wild Duck*, published in November of the following year, was largely one of bewilderment, although it was produced without delay in all the major Scandinavian venues. While the 'original sin' of the drama, the housemaid made pregnant by her master and married off to a convenient dupe, echoes that of *Ghosts*, Ibsen's use of symbolism appeared to sit uneasily with the naturalistic dialogue, and indeed still troubles modern audiences.

However, Ibsen was moving away from the concerns of the 'problem play' towards a more personal, oblique utterance, and the controversy which dogged his work scarcely lessened with the publication of *Rosmersholm*, in November 1886. Especially noteworthy for the creation of Rebecca West, one of Ibsen's most compelling characters, its witches' brew of ingredients even included incest, and it caused a minor scandal.

Ibsen's reputation was by now unassailable, however, and in Germany particularly, the innovative productions of the Saxe-Meiningen company had won him an eager following. In England, the enthusiasm of Edmund Gosse, and later William Archer, ensured that several of his plays were at least published in English, but the first significant staging of his work in London had to wait until June 1889, with the Novelty Theatre production of *A Doll's House*.

Meanwhile, *The Lady from the Sea* fared well enough at the box office, with simultaneous premières in Kristiania and in German at Weimar, on 12 February, 1889, though again its complex amalgam of dreamy symbolism, evolutionary theory, and the daily routine of the Wangel household in northern Norway, tended to confuse audiences, and is still something of an obstacle to production.

Hedda Gabler, premièred in Munich at the Residenztheater in January 1891, is now, along with *A Doll's House*, Ibsen's most popular play, but it attracted fierce criticism in its day, largely on account of the character of Hedda herself. Arguably Ibsen's finest creation, Hedda's contempt for the sacred roles of wife and mother seemed the more offensive in that Ibsen provided no explanation for it, no inherited moral taint, and she continues to unnerve us even today, like a glimpse into the abyss.

In that same year, 1891, there were no fewer than five London productions of Ibsen plays, including *Hedda Gabler*; and the publication of George Bernard Shaw's seminal critique, *The Quintessence of Ibsenism*, helped assure his place in the permanent English repertoire. Ibsen himself returned to Norway in July, a national hero, though he suffered the indignity of hearing his achievement disparaged by the rising young novelist Knut Hamsun, at a public lecture in October.

In his declining years, Ibsen increasingly sought the company of young female admirers, and his relationships with Emilie Bardach, Helene Raff, and finally Hildur Andersen, find their way into his later plays, notably *The Master Builder*, in which Ibsen also returns to the theme of self, which had inspired his early masterpieces, *Brand* and *Peer Gynt*. The burden of fame, the generational conflict between age and youth, Ibsen's personal concerns, are explored in the relationship between the successful middle-aged architect Solness and the twenty-something 'free spirit' Hilde Wangel. Although the all-pervasive tower metaphor puzzled some critics, given that Freud had still to explain such things, the play was an instant success, going on from its première in Berlin in January 1893, to productions in Scandinavia, Paris, Chicago and London within the year.

Ibsen's next play, *Little Eyolf*, despite having the distinction of a public reading in English, at the Haymarket Theatre in December 1893, even before it was published in Copenhagen, has enjoyed little success on the stage, where its mixed modes of realism and symbolism can fail to blend, with unintentionally comic results. However, *John Gabriel Borkman*, published three years later, and premièred in Helsinki in January 1897, achieves in prose the poetic grandeur of *Brand*. The play is drawn in part from Ibsen's own experience of humiliating dependency, in the wake of his father's financial ruin, and explores Ibsen's cherished themes, the corrupting influence of materialism, personal freedom and self-doubt, and marital disharmony.

Ibsen was now permanently resident in Kristiania, venerated wherever he went, and his seventieth birthday, on 20 March, 1898, was the occasion for widespread rejoicing. His collected works were in preparation in both Denmark and Germany, and his international fame rivalled that of Tolstoy. It is fitting, therefore, that Ibsen's last play, *When We Dead Awaken*, should have been premièred on 15 January, 1900, in effect launching the next century, at Kristiania's new National Theatre, the confident expression of that Norwegian identity which Ibsen and Bjørnson, whose statues graced its entrance, did so much to promote.

Finally, like almost all of Ibsen's plays, *When We Dead Awaken* is a response to the author's psychic needs, part confession, part exorcism, and it can be argued that the ageing sculptor Rubek's return to his first inspiration, Irene, now confined in a sanatorium, represents Ibsen's feelings of guilt over his neglect of his wife Suzannah, and his belated acknowledgement that she had been the real sustaining force behind his work. The tone of *When We Dead Awaken* is accordingly elegiac, an appropriate coda to Ibsen's long career. Two months later, in March 1900, he suffered the first of a series of strokes which was to lead to his death, in Kristiania, on 23 May, 1906.

The Lady from the Sea: **What Happens in the Play**

The action of the play takes place in and near the house of Doctor Wangel, at the head of a fjord in northern Norway. Wangel is married to Ellida, considerably younger than himself, and the daughter of a lighthouse keeper. She is Wangel's second wife, and apart from being seen as an outsider by her two grown-up stepdaughters, she also yearns desperately for the sea, from which she feels cut off. Wangel and Ellida have lost a child of their own, three years before, as a consequence of which Ellida, believing that their son's death was mysteriously linked to a former lover, whom she gave up to marry Wangel, no longer sleeps with her husband, and seems alienated from the family.

As the play opens, Ballested, the local jack-of-all-trades, is helping to hang a flag, and Wangel's elder daughter Bolette is setting out flowers, ostensibly preparing for the arrival of her former tutor, Arnholm. A visitor to the area, Lyngstrand, asks Ballested about the painting he is working on, which he says is to feature a dying mermaid, stranded on dry land, and adds that the image was inspired by the Doctor's wife. As a steamer bringing tourists appears in the distance, and Ballested goes off to welcome them, Wangel's younger daughter Hilde emerges from the house. Upon enquiry, she tells Lyngstrand that they are celebrating her mother's birthday, and he naturally assumes she means Ellida.

Lyngstrand then leaves, and Dr Wangel returns home from his rounds. He notes the preparations, and realises that the girls are using Arnholm's visit as an excuse to mark his deceased first wife's birthday, which Ellida is sure to feel as a slight. Arnholm then arrives, and Wangel recounts his family situation, including the death of their baby son, and Ellida's present disturbed state of mind. Wangel tells him that swimming in the fjord, which Ellida does every day, regardless of the weather, is her only relief, and Arnholm, who knew her in her youth, avers that Ellida has always been obsessed by the sea. The local people, according to Wangel, even call her 'the mermaid', and as if in confirmation of that, Ellida then appears from her daily swim, still dripping wet.

Ellida and Arnholm, left alone, recall their past life, and it emerges that Arnholm had once been in love with her, but she had rejected him for someone else. She is reluctant to say more, and they are in any case interrupted by the return of Lyngstrand, now bearing a bouquet of flowers, which he mistakenly presents to Ellida in honour of her birthday. Ellida is briefly nonplussed, but soon recovers. In the course of conversation, Lyngstrand mentions his ambition to become an artist, and create a sculpture of a woman whose peace is disturbed by the spirit of her drowned sailor husband, to whom she has been unfaithful, watching over her as she sleeps. Lyngstrand tells her the image is based on a real experience – he himself had been a seaman, and had witnessed a fellow-sailor, supposedly American, becoming extremely agitated on reading a report of a marriage in a Norwegian newspaper. The sailor had then uttered some dark threats, vowing to return to claim his faithless wife, even if he should perish at sea. Ellida is evidently disturbed, and on further questioning, Lyngstrand tells her that the man was most likely drowned, when their vessel was wrecked in the English Channel not long after.

Lyngstrand leaves, and Arnholm, observing Ellida's agitation, assumes it is because of the birthday events, from which she inevitably feels excluded. She denies this, and promises to confide in him later. Her husband and stepdaughters then return, and Ellida, despite some initial awkwardness, puts on a brave face for the celebrations.

Act Two is set on a wooded hill behind the town. Lyngstrand and the Wangel sisters are climbing up it to enjoy the view, and Hilde, irritated at Lyngstrand's snail-like pace, learns from Bolette that the artist is terminally ill with lung cancer. When Lyngstrand eventually appears, he makes light of his illness, and Hilde confesses to her sister that she finds him fascinating because he is doomed, yet still burns with ambition. The sisters go on to discuss Arnholm, and their stepmother, rather disparagingly, before they are interrupted by the arrival of the rest of the group. The girls then conduct Lyngstrand and Arnholm to another part of the hill, while Doctor Wangel and Ellida have a serious discussion about their failing marriage. Wangel understands Ellida's homesickness for the sea, and offers to move the family to the coast, to restore her peace of mind. Ellida is surprised and touched, but tells him that not even that would cure her malaise.

Ellida reminds Wangel that she had been engaged to another man, when he first asked her to marry him. He had believed it to be Arnholm, but in fact it had been a seaman on an American ship, whom she knew first as Friman, later as Johnston, and who had reputedly murdered his captain, and fled to escape justice. Johnston had been as sea-obsessed as Ellida herself, and at their enforced parting, he had joined their rings together and flung them into the water, as a sign of their betrothal, and union with the sea. Later, however, Ellida had written to Johnston, trying to end the relationship, but his replies made it clear that he still regarded her as his wife, and promised to return for her. Ellida tells Wangel that Johnston has some mysterious power over her, which she felt most intensely when she was pregnant with Wangel's child. It is not that she loves Johnston, she insists – in fact, he inspires her with terror.

The couple are then joined by Lyngstrand, and Ellida asks him for more information on the strange sailor he had earlier mentioned. She discovers that the date of the shipwreck, in which Johnston presumably drowned, coincides with the first of his apparitions to her. At their most terrifying, she experiences visions of him wearing a pearl stick-pin, like a dead fish's eye, and she tells Wangel that their own child's eyes, before his death, used to change colour with the moods of the sea, exactly like Johnston's. Wangel dismisses all this as a figment of her imagination, but Ellida is adamant, and finally confesses it to be the reason she has ceased to be a wife to him, before she runs off in despair.

Act Three takes place in a corner of Doctor Wangel's garden, beside a goldfish pond. Lyngstrand and Hilde are fishing, until Arnholm arrives to talk with Bolette, who is sitting sewing nearby. Bolette confides her scholarly ambitions to Arnholm, but admits that they will remain only a dream while she stays at home, acting as unpaid housekeeper to her father. Bolette sees her situation, indeed, as similar to that of the goldfish, imprisoned in their stagnant pond, and is overjoyed when Arnholm encourages her and promises to speak to her father on her behalf. He is just nerving himself to say something else, when they are joined by Ellida.

Ellida has been out walking with her husband, and is now in a more relaxed frame of mind. The sight of a steamer arriving prompts her to express her longing to make a sea voyage, and they go on to discuss human evolution, speculating on which is man's 'natural' element, land or sea. Arnholm agrees with Ellida that perhaps the wrong evolutionary path has been chosen, but it is too late to change now. Ellida argues that that is the reason why humanity in general is so profoundly unhappy. Arnholm and Bolette then go off in search of Wangel, leaving Ellida by herself. Suddenly, a stranger appears, and after some hesitation, Ellida recognises him by his remarkable eyes – it is Johnston.

Ellida is terrified, but the Stranger insists he means her no harm – he has simply come to take her away with him. He ignores Ellida's protestations that she is now another man's wife, and appears almost on the point of hypnotising her, when Doctor Wangel returns, and Ellida

begs her husband to save her. The Stranger then tells
Wangel that he regards Ellida as his, bound to him by the
ceremony of the linked rings, thrown into the sea, even
though he acknowledges that she is legally married to
Wangel. Ellida insists she never wants to see the Stranger
again, but he extorts a promise that she will meet him one
last time, the next night, alone, when she will give him
her final decision. If she still rejects him, of her own free
will, he will disappear from her life. After the Stranger
leaves, Wangel tries to comfort Ellida, who seems oddly
torn between her desire to be rid of the Stranger, and her
fear of losing him forever. Wangel suggests reporting him
to the police, as a fugitive murderer, but Ellida begs him
not to – the Stranger's place is the sea. At the same time,
she appeals to Wangel to save her from him. Lyngstrand
and Hilde then appear, having just passed the Stranger on
the road, and Lyngstrand confirms it is the same
American sailor he had known, and who had threatened
to punish his faithless wife. Ellida once more pleads with
Wangel to save her, this time from herself.

At the beginning of Act Four, Bolette and Lyngstrand are
sitting in the conservatory, while Ballested is painting
outside in the garden, watched by Hilde. Lyngstrand
begins talking about marriage, theorising that a wife
inevitably subdues her own personality to that of her
husband, as the years pass, but rejects the counter-
proposition, put by Bolette, on the grounds that an artist's
wife has a duty to dedicate herself totally to his art. In his
defence, Lyngstrand refers to his illness, which he
confidently believes he will recover from, inspired by her
support. At that point, they are joined by Arnholm, who

enquires after Ellida, and is told that she has locked herself in her room. Doctor Wangel then appears, and Bolette and Lyngstrand go out into the garden, leaving Wangel and Arnholm to continue their discussion about Ellida. Wangel blames himself for failing to recognise that his wife could not survive without the sea, and confesses himself unable to account for the Stranger's mysterious power over her. Arnholm quizzes him about Ellida's fixation with the Stranger's eyes, and their alleged similarity with those of his dead child, but Wangel answers him evasively. However, he does admit that her neurosis first took hold at the same time the Stranger began making his way home, as confirmed by Lyngstrand.

Ellida then appears, and seeks Wangel's assurance that he will not leave the house that day. Arnholm goes off in search of the girls, and Ellida and Wangel discuss the events of the previous day in more detail. She is forced to admit that the Stranger does not in fact resemble the figure of her nightmares, and Wangel suggests that the real person has now erased the other from her mind. Ellida then tries to explain her feelings rationally, and confesses to having married Wangel in the first place for security, so that their marriage has never been a true union, entered into from choice. She appeals to Wangel to release her, to annul what she now regards as a marriage of convenience, and allow her to depart with the Stranger if she wishes. He asks her if she loves the Stranger – she has no answer, only that she feels she belongs with him, the root of her terror. Wangel then refuses to let her go into the unknown with the Stranger, a course of action fraught with peril, but promises to release her, if that is her will, as soon as the Stranger has gone. When Arnholm and the girls return, Wangel announces that Ellida is going home to the sea, and for the first time, Ellida is made aware that her stepdaughters might need her. Finally, they drink a farewell toast to the 'lady from the sea'.

Act Five returns to the setting of the goldfish pond. Arnholm, Lyngstrand and the girls are boating, when Ballested appears, on his way to play in a local band, welcoming an English tourist steamer. Ellida and Wangel enter, uneasily awaiting the fateful meeting with the Stranger, with Ellida still undecided. After they go out, Arnholm and Bolette discuss the latter's plans to leave home to study, and he offers to assist her. She readily accepts, but when it emerges that he wishes her to marry him, she immediately changes her mind. After some further discussion, however, she agrees, but asks him to keep their engagement secret. They leave, just as Hilde and Lyngstrand arrive. Hilde guesses that Arnholm has been declaring his love to Bolette, but Lyngstrand insists nothing can come of it, believing that Bolette's promise to support him in some way ruled out any other commitment, although he himself could not contemplate marriage until he has achieved his artistic goal. However, Hilde will be Bolette's present age by then, and he suggests that *they* might marry.

Their hypothetical courtship is interrupted by the arrival of the English steamer, and the return of Ellida and Wangel, who send Hilde and Lyngstrand to the pier, while they await the Stranger. Wangel offers to confront him alone, but Ellida insists on remaining. When the Stranger appears, he asks Ellida to come with him, of her own free will. Wangel tells him to leave the country before he is arrested for murder, but the Stranger produces a pistol, and swears he will never be taken alive. Ellida tells Wangel that while he may be able to restrain her from leaving, physically, he can never possess her spirit – that will always be drawn irresistibly to the unknown. Sadly, Wangel accepts defeat, and agrees to release her. His love for her is such that he is even prepared to yield her up to the Stranger, if she chooses to go, on her own responsibility. Ellida is stopped in her tracks – the idea of responsibility is something new to her, and she realises that she is also free to reject the Stranger. Crushed, the Stranger departs for good, leaving Ellida and Wangel to discuss a changed relationship, in which she can become a true wife, and the mother of their children. Mermaids die out of their element, as Ballested says, but human beings, able to exercise free will, and take responsibility for their actions, can acclimatise.

The Lady from the Sea

Ibsen wrote preliminary sketches for *The Lady from the Sea* in 1860, soon after the success of *A Doll's House*, but then put the play aside for eight years, while he wrote *Ghosts*, *An Enemy of the People*, *The Wild Duck* and *Rosmersholm*. He began the final version in the summer of 1888, and it was published in November that year.

Like *A Doll's House* and *Hedda Gabler* (which followed *The Lady from the Sea* in 1890), this play is a study of the differing expectations of the partners in a dysfunctional relationship, and of the way other relationships, past and present, impinge on those expectations and force change in one or both of the partners. In *A Doll's House*, an outside event (Krogstad's attempted blackmail) forces Nora to reassess her relationship to her husband Helmer and her position in the household; the play concerns her attempt to make him understand her new perception of herself, and ends when she leaves him and he faces the possibility that he too may have to change. In *Hedda Gabler* it is Hedda's husband Tesman who grows and changes as a result of outside events (the return of Løvborg and the need to reconstitute his destroyed manuscript after his suicide): Hedda, unable to change, turns her despair and disdain inwards and shoots herself. In *The Lady from the Sea*, outside events (the return of the Stranger, and his demand that Ellida go away with him) change both leading characters and even leave us reflecting how the changes might affect their relationship once the play is over.

The play's origin is a Scandinavian folk-tale about a sea-woman who falls in love with a human, comes to land and sheds her sea-skin, then, unable to find it and return to the sea, despairs and dies. Hans Andersen wrote a straightforward, fairy-tale version, the naturalistic simplicity of whose telling only deepens the mood of bleakness and mystery. Ibsen, by contrast, layers the original story with ironies, secrets and deceptions, so that the play continually – even after the final twist of plot – has the effect not of certainty but of suggestion, of evocation, rather than affirmation. Even the dramatic form he chooses is ironical. The play opens in, and continually returns to, a mood of relaxed, autumnal comedy, Chekhovian in tone. Ballested,

that enthusiastic jack-of-all-trades, and the young people
Hilde and Lyngstrand are the chief contributors of that
mood, and the play's dynamic changes each time they
appear. But, with the exception of the Stranger, that figure
of remorseless dark, the main characters also make
amiable, inconsequential conversation whose undercurrents
become apparent only as the action proceeds. Characters
talk of how the days grow darker and ice gradually forms
on the sea-ways as summer gives way to winter –
metaphors for the psychological darkening and closing-in
which overtake the light-hearted mood established by the
first twenty minutes of the action.

If the mood of Act One were sustained throughout, *The
Lady from the Sea* would be a genial melodrama about a
kind husband who rescues his wife from mental torment.
But scene by scene, almost speech by speech, Ibsen
unpeels the onion-skins of his main characters and shows
that none of them is what he or she seems. For all the
superficial courtesies and polite manners of the Wangel
family, its dysfunction can hardly be overstated. The
teenager Hilde - prototype of the adult character of the
same name in *The Master Builder* – flirts maliciously, edgily,
with a man she knows is dying: she seems more excited
(her word) by the fact that Lyngstrand's life will never be
fulfilled than by the fatuous theories and ambitions he
articulates; she plays with him like cat with mouse. Her
sister Bolette at first plays a saintly, self-denying role on
the periphery of events, sewing, embroidering, bringing
cool drinks, smiling, soothing. Ambition and self-image
seem to have been replaced in her by a kind of wistful
acceptance of her life's futility – she says she is like a pet

goldfish in a pond. But as soon as the chance of escape is offered, she snatches at it ruthlessly, exploiting the proposal of a man for whom she feels no affection, making conditions of the marriage that she is to be allowed to see the world and study at his expense. Both sisters revere their dead mother to the extent of decorating the house with flowers and flying a flag every year on her birthday, to the exclusion of their father's second wife – and their father connives in this.

The two characters at the heart of the drama, those on whom change will chiefly operate, are unpeeled most of all. Neither is anything like what he or she seems at first, second, or even third appearance. In Act One Wangel appears to be a mild, affectionate father and husband, making the best of a 'difficult' second marriage. But the more we find out about him – and perhaps to his own surprise as much as ours – the less estimable he seems. Without realising it, and without ever raising his voice or clenching his fist, he is a domestic tyrant, unhappy unless his needs and wishes override all others. He married his second wife Ellida – so he tells her, and us – not for love but because he was lonely: affection came unexpectedly and later. He 'has his little ways', needs to be pampered (something at which his first wife was adept), is fond of a drink – and when Ellida is unable to cope, gives her drugs to calm her rather than cure her. His unassuming politeness masks inability to make any genuine emotional or social bridge: his doctor's manner, his bedside manner, has become his way of dealing with every situation.

This character, once revealed, is utterly changed as the play proceeds. The Stranger threatens not merely

Wangel's comfort but his whole self-image, and the play charts the way he copes with this. He begins by pouring scorn on Ellida's obsession, then tries to bully her and the Stranger out of their relationship. He believes, and acts as if she also believes, that she is mad and should leave all decisions to him. It is only when this fails, when he is forced to consider her situation from her point of view, that the thing he has always been assuming, and claiming, becomes reality, and he discovers in himself the capacity for genuine love: as he says in Act Four: 'For me, what terrifies, what I long for – it lies in you yourself'. That realisation leads him to make the ultimate offer of self-immolation, giving up what he loves *because* he loves it – in Act Five he says, 'When the case is desperate, a doctor's brave' – and this self-denial ironically brings about exactly the result he longs for, but which his unchanged self could never have achieved: Ellida stays.

At the heart of the whole play is the character of Ellida, the 'lady from the sea'. In passing, she is not a 'mermaid'. The word for mermaid, for example the one in Ballested's painting, is *havfru*, literally 'sea-wife'; Ellida is *fruen fra havet*, 'the (married) woman from the sea'. Wangel says that she *is* the sea, that her mind is like the sea, and that her character ebbs and flows like tides or currents. The critic James Agate wrote that when the great actress Eleanora Duse played the role, 'terror and ecstasy (swept) across her face… as if this were not present stress, but havoc remembered of past time. Her features (had) the placidity of long grief; so many storms (had) broken over them that nothing (could) disturb again this sea of calm distress' – words which evoke the character as much as the performer. Early audiences were baffled by Ellida, unsettled by the 'occultism' they saw in the part and convinced that 'insanity' was not a fit subject for realistic dramatic presentation. Modern productions, delving deeper into both Ellida's and Wangel's characters and their relationship, tend to present Ellida not as insane, but as driven almost beyond endurance by her domestic situation – and by the yearning shared by other Ibsen heroines: to find the doorway which will take them from the repression of their upbringing and surroundings into existential freedom. If her distress had been caused entirely by the Stranger, it would have been resolvable only if she immolated herself by going with him. But although it is focused on him, it actually arises from her relationship with Wangel, and her almost instant 'recovery' when he declares her free to take responsibility for her own life is not a plot-contrivance, but a moment of radiant character-affirmation, sun breaking through clouds.

In the play's tide-like ebb and flow, darkness and light constantly refract one another. Psychological gloom is balanced by cheerfulness, hope and happiness. The young people fish, go walking, sailing, dance and joke. Arnholm and Lyngstrand, though each in his own way is a pathetic character, bring new life to both the town and the Wangel family; the positiveness of their outlook, undiminished by events, is constantly refreshing. Wangel is not a charmless bully, but capable of enormous tenderness and emotional sympathy. Under all the apparent aloneness and alienation of his and Ellida's relationship, we (and they) sense a possibility of comfort with one another, of accommodation, and this suggests that the confrontation of truth forced on them by the Stranger will lead to the fulfilled future relationship to which they both aspire.

Some authorities have condemned the apparent abruptness of the play's conclusion. Both Wangel's declaration that Ellida is free to choose her own destiny, and her answer, that she chooses to stay with him, take no more than a handful of ordinary-seeming words. In both Ibsen's time and later, scholars have claimed that this curtness is a sign of surrender to the melodramatic tradition, that he is abandoning his characters' psychological complexity for a cheap-trick happy ending, and that this is an uncharacteristic and deplorable lapse from dramaturgical competence. But the suddenness of transformation can also be seen as like the moment when the statue comes to life in Shakespeare's *The Winter's Tale*, and moves the play, in a similar way, on to a level of meaning quite different from the rest of the action, Ibsen's last stroke of genius in turning a simple sea-woman folk story into a layered and complex psycho-drama, and then into transcendental fairy-tale.

Kenneth McLeish, 1996

The Lady from the Sea in Performance:

Following its simultaneous première at the Kristiania Theatre, and the Hoftheater, Weimar, on February 12, 1889, *The Lady from the Sea* was staged in Copenhagen, Berlin, Stockholm and Helsinki, within the next few weeks. The first London production took place at Terry's Theatre in May 1891, and the following year, Lugné-Poë staged the play in Paris, at the Théâtre Moderne, taking the role of Wangel himself. The success of any production of *The Lady from the Sea* depends heavily on the interpretation of Ellida Wangel, and the role has attracted some of the finest actresses in Europe. Lydia Yavorskaya introduced the work to Russian audiences at the New Theatre in St Petersburg, in January 1903, and the great Sarah Bernhardt first played Ibsen's 'mermaid' at Sens, in 1904. However, arguably the most celebrated Ellida of her generation was Eleanora Duse, first in Turin, in 1921, and later in London and New York. Closer to our own day, Vanessa Redgrave's acclaimed performance as Ellida at the Circle in the Square Theatre, New York, in 1976, and the Round House Theatre in London, in 1979, under Michael Elliott's direction, is still seen as a benchmark.

Further Reading

In addition to a valuable introduction to *The Lady from the Sea*, Volume VII of the Oxford *Ibsen*, ed. James McFarlane, Oxford University Press, 1966, includes detailed scholarly notes on Ibsen's text. Edited by the same author, *The Cambridge Companion to Ibsen*, Cambridge University Press, 1994, is a varied collection of essays by a distinguished international cast, while George B. Bryan's *An Ibsen Companion*, Greenwood Press, Westport, Conn., 1984, is a very useful guide, in dictionary format, to Ibsen's life and work. A similar function is served by Michael Meyer's compact little *Ibsen on File*, Methuen, 1985. Meyer's three-volume *Henrik Ibsen*, revised in 1992, and also available in a single, condensed volume, is justly regarded as the authoritative work on Ibsen's life, and the theatre and politics of the day. The revised version of Halvdan Koht's *Life of Ibsen*, translated by Haugen and Santaniello, and published by Benjamin Blom, Inc., New York, 1971, despite its venerable age (first published in 1928 to mark Ibsen's centennial) is also worth reading, while Robert Ferguson's *Henrik Ibsen - A New Biography*, Richard Cohen Books, 1996, is a fascinating warts-and-all portrayal of a deeply troubled spirit.

Ibsen: Key Dates

1828   Born 20 March in Skien, south-east Norway.

1835   Father's business fails, family moves to Venstøp.

1844   Ibsen leaves school, becomes apprentice pharmacist in Grimstad.

1846   Aged eighteen, Ibsen fathers illegitimate son, by housemaid Else Sofie Jensdatter.

1849   First play, *Catiline*, rejected by Kristiania Danish Theatre.

1850   Fails university entrance exam. Première of *The Warrior's Barrow*, 26 September, Kristiania Theatre.

1851   Appointed writer-in-residence at Bergen Norwegian Theatre.

1853   *St. John's Night*.

1854   *The Warrior's Barrow* revised.

1855   *Lady Inger of Østråt*.

1856   *The Feast at Solhaug*.

1857   Final contracted play for Bergen Theatre, *Olaf Liljekrans*. Appointed artistic director at Norwegian Theatre in Kristiania.

1858   Marries Suzannah Thoresen, 18 June. *The Vikings at Helgeland*, 24 November.

1862   Norwegian Theatre fails, Ibsen tours Western Norway, collecting folklore.

1864   *The Pretenders*, 17 January, at Kristiania Theatre.

1864	Leaves Norway, travels to Rome, via Copenhagen, Lübeck, Berlin and Vienna.
1866	*Brand*.
1867	*Peer Gynt*.
1868	Moves from Rome to settle in Dresden.
1869	Invited to represent Norway at opening of Suez Canal. *The League of Youth*.
1871	Publication of collected poems.
1873	*Emperor and Galilean*. Première of *Love's Comedy*, Kristiania, 24 November.
1874	Edvard Grieg invited to supply incidental music for *Peer Gynt*.
1875	Leaves Dresden to settle in Munich.
1876	*Peer Gynt* premièred, Kristiania, 24 February.
1877	*The Pillars of Society*.
1879	*A Doll's House*.
1881	*Ghosts*.
1882	*An Enemy of the People*.
1884	*The Wild Duck*.
1886	*Rosmersholm*.
1887	Meininger Company presents *Ghosts*, 23 December.
1888	*The Lady from the Sea*.
1890	Antoine's Théâtre Libre presents *Ghosts*, Paris, 29 May. *Hedda Gabler*.
1891	Returns to Norway, settles in Kristiania.
1892	*The Master Builder*.
1894	*Little Eyolf*.
1896	*John Gabriel Borkman*.
1899	*Hedda Gabler* produced at Moscow Art Theatre. *When We Dead Awaken*.
1900	Suffers first of a series of strokes, 15 March.
1906	Dies 23 May, Kristiania.

THE LADY FROM THE SEA

Characters

DOCTOR WANGEL
ELLIDA WANGEL, *his second wife*
BOLETTE, *his elder daughter from a previous marriage*
HILDE, *her sister (in her teens)*
ARNHOLM, *a private tutor*
LYNGSTRAND
BALLESTED
STRANGER

Young people of the town, tourists, summer visitors

The action takes place in summer, in a small fjordside town in Northern Norway. There are five acts.

Translator's note: to help cope in English with the complexities of Norwegian forms of address, I have given Wangel a first name: Edvard. This is used only by Ellida; in the original, each time, she calls him 'Wangel'.

See page 127 for a guide to the Pronunciation of Proper Names.

ACT ONE

The garden of WANGEL's *house. The garden surrounds the house. Left, spacious verandah, with a flagpole beside it. Right, arbour with table and chairs. At rear, hedge and small gate, leading to a tree-lined road along the shore. Between the trees we can see the fjord, with mountains beyond.*

Warm, dazzlingly bright summer morning. BALLESTED *is standing by the flagpole, fiddling with the cord. He is middle-aged and wears a velvet jacket and a broad-brimmed artist's hat. The flag is lying on the ground. A little way off, easel with canvas, camp-stool, brushes, palette and paint-box.*

Enter BOLETTE *to the verandah, from the open garden-door of the house. She has a large vase of flowers, and puts it on the table.*

BOLETTE. Well, Ballested? Any luck?

BALLESTED. It was caught, that's all. Expecting visitors?

BOLETTE. Mr Arnholm, any minute. He arrived in town last night.

BALLESTED. Didn't you have a tutor, once, called Arnholm?

BOLETTE. The same man.

BALLESTED. In town again?

BOLETTE. That's why we're flying the flag.

BALLESTED. Yes of course.

BOLETTE goes in. Pause. LYNGSTRAND comes down the road and stops by the hedge, intrigued by the easel and painting things. He is young, slender, frail-looking and neatly but shabbily dressed.

LYNGSTRAND. Good morning.

BALLESTED (*turning*). Morning. (*Hoisting the flag.*) *There* we go, *up* it goes.

He fastens the cord and goes to busy himself at the easel.

A very good morning, whoever you are. I don't think we've –

LYNGSTRAND. You're a painter.

BALLESTED. Any reason why not?

LYNGSTRAND. No, no. Mind if I come in?

BALLESTED. You want to look?

LYNGSTRAND. If that's all right.

BALLESTED. There's nothing to see, so far. But come in anyway, and welcome.

LYNGSTRAND. Thank you.

He comes in through the gate. BALLESTED is painting.

BALLESTED. It's a view of the fjord, the islands.

LYNGSTRAND. I see that.

BALLESTED. I haven't put any people in yet. No models in town, for love or money.

LYNGSTRAND. You're putting people in?

BALLESTED. Well, one. By this rock in the foreground. A dying mermaid.

LYNGSTRAND. Why dying?

BALLESTED. She's come to land, and she can't get back. So she's lying in the shallows, dying, like a fish out of water. If you get the idea.

LYNGSTRAND. Mm.

BALLESTED. Mrs Wangel, the doctor's wife, there in the house, gave me the idea.

LYNGSTRAND. What are you calling it?

BALLESTED. 'Mermaid's End.'

LYNGSTRAND. Good title. Interesting idea.

BALLESTED (*looking at him*). You're an artist?

LYNGSTRAND. A painter?

BALLESTED. Yes.

LYNGSTRAND. No. Sculptor. Or will be, one day. My name's Hans Lyngstrand.

BALLESTED. A sculptor, one day? Nothing wrong with that. I've seen you before, haven't I? In the street, in town. Have you been here long?

LYNGSTRAND. A couple of weeks. But I'm here for the summer.

BALLESTED. Sand, sea and sunshine?

LYNGSTRAND. I'm here for my health.

BALLESTED. Not serious, I hope?

LYNGSTRAND. No, no. A kind of . . . breathlessness.

BALLESTED. Nothing to worry about. See a good doctor.

LYNGSTRAND. I was wondering . . . Doctor Wangel . . .

BALLESTED. He's your man.

He looks off, left.

Another steamer. Seething with tourists. This place has gone up in the world, these last few years.

LYNGSTRAND. Tours up and down the fjord.

BALLESTED. And people stopping here. The town's crammed every summer. An invasion. I hope they don't change the place.

LYNGSTRAND. You were born here?

BALLESTED. No, no. Accal . . . acclimatised. Used to the place. After all these years.

LYNGSTRAND. How many?

BALLESTED. Seventeen, eighteen . . . I worked in the theatre. Skive's company. We came here on tour, ran out of cash, the company split up . . .

LYNGSTRAND. And you stayed?

BALLESTED. Got it in one. Not to mention up in the world. In those days I painted scenery, not landscapes.

Enter BOLETTE *with a rocking-chair, which she puts on the verandah. She speaks back into the house.*

BOLETTE. Hilde, see if you can find Papa's footstool, the embroidered one.

LYNGSTRAND *goes to the verandah to speak to her.*

LYNGSTRAND. Miss Wangel, good morning.

BOLETTE (*over the balustrade*). Mr Lyngstrand. Good morning. Excuse me a moment. I –

Exit into the house.

BALLESTED. You know them?

LYNGSTRAND. Not really. The girls, I've met them once or twice at parties. And I met Mrs Wangel the other day at the Viewpoint, when the band was playing. She said I ought to call.

BALLESTED. Good idea. Get to know them.

LYNGSTRAND. I've been meaning to. A formal call. The problem was, what reason . . . ?

BALLESTED. Who needs a reason?

He looks out left again.

Damn it!

He starts gathering his things.

The boat's docking already. I ought to be at the hotel. The visitors, some of them may require my services. Barber, *friseur* . . . *you* know.

LYNGSTRAND. You're really versatile.

BALLESTED. You have to be. Accal . . . acclimatised. Several strings to the bow. It's a very small town. If you ever need anything in the hair line, shampoo, pomade, just ask for Ballested, the dancing-master.

LYNGSTRAND. Dancing-master?

BALLESTED. President of the Music Club. You name it. We're playing at the Viewpoint this evening. Excuse me.

Exit with his things, through the gate and off left. Enter from the house, HILDE *with the footstool,* BOLETTE *with more flowers.* LYNGSTRAND *bows to* HILDE, *who doesn't bow back.*

HILDE. Bolette said you'd risked it. Coming in today.

LYNGSTRAND. Yes. I took the liberty. In through the gate.

HILDE. Been for a walk, have you?

LYNGSTRAND. No, not for a walk.

HILDE. A swim, then?

LYNGSTRAND. A dip, that's all. I saw your mother. Going into her bathing-house.

HILDE. Who was?

LYNGSTRAND. She was. Your mother.

HILDE. Was she?

She puts the footstool down in front of the rocking-chair.

BOLETTE (*to change the subject*). Did you see Papa's boat, out on the fjord?

LYNGSTRAND. A sailing-dinghy, making for shore.

BOLETTE. That's Papa. He's been seeing patients on the islands.

She arranges things on the table.

LYNGSTRAND *goes on to the first step up to the verandah.*

LYNGSTRAND. Just look at all those flowers.

BOLETTE. They're pretty, aren't they?

LYNGSTRAND. Magnificent. It looks ready for a party. A family party.

HILDE. That's because it is.

LYNGSTRAND. I guessed. Someone's birthday? Your father's?

BOLETTE (*warningly to* HILDE). Ahem.

HILDE (*heedless*). No, Mama's.

LYNGSTRAND. Mrs Wangel's.

BOLETTE (*crossly, aside*). For Heaven's sake, Hilde!

HILDE (*the same*). Leave me alone! (*to* LYNGSTRAND) I suppose you're going for lunch now.

LYNGSTRAND (*stepping down*). A man must eat.

HILDE. I bet they do you well at that hotel.

LYNGSTRAND. Oh, I've left the hotel. Too expensive.

HILDE. Where are you now?

LYNGSTRAND. Boarding house. Mrs Jensen's.

HILDE. Which Mrs Jensen?

LYNGSTRAND. The midwife.

HILDE. Mr Lyngstrand!

LYNGSTRAND. I'm sorry, I didn't mean to –

HILDE. Mean to what?

LYNGSTRAND. Embarrass you.

HILDE (*witheringly*). I don't know *what* you mean.

LYNGSTRAND. No. No. Well, ladies, time to say
goodbye.

BOLETTE *comes to the top of the steps.*

BOLETTE. Goodbye, Mr Lyngstrand. We're sorry today's
not . . . But some other time . . . when you've time . . .
if you want to . . . call and see Papa and . . . the rest
of us.

LYNGSTRAND. Oh I will. Thank you. I really will.

*He bows, goes out through the garden gate, bows again as he
goes off left along the road.*

HILDE (*sotto voce*). Adieu, mossieu! Give Ma Jensen a
great big kiss.

BOLETTE (*in a low voice, shaking her arm*). Hilde! Are you
mad? He'll hear you!

HILDE. See if I care.

BOLETTE (*looking off right*). Here comes Papa.

WANGEL *comes right along the road, in outdoor clothes and carrying a doctor's bag.*

WANGEL. Here I am, girls.

He comes through the gate. BOLETTE *goes to greet him in the garden.*

BOLETTE. Papa, it's good to see you.

HILDE (*also going to him*). Have you finished now today, Papa?

WANGEL. Surgery later, and then I'm done. Tell me, d'you know if Arnholm's arrived yet?

BOLETTE. Last night. We sent to ask at the hotel.

WANGEL. You haven't seen him yourselves?

BOLETTE. He'll come this afternoon.

WANGEL. That's right, he will.

HILDE *pulls him round.*

HILDE. Papa . . . look! Look!

WANGEL (*looking at the verandah*). Yes, darling. Very pretty.

BOLETTE. You really think so?

WANGEL. Oh yes. Is . . . are we alone in the house?

HILDE. Yes, *she's* gone –

BOLETTE (*quickly*). Mother's gone bathing.

WANGEL *smiles and pats her head. Then he says, with some hesitation:*

WANGEL. The thing is, girls . . . Are you going to leave it like this all day? All this . . . a flag, even?

HILDE. Oh Papa, of course we are.

WANGEL. The thing is . . . I . . . you . . .

BOLETTE (*with a smile*). You see, it's entirely in Mr Arnholm's honour. Such a dear friend, coming visiting after all these years . . .

HILDE (*smiling, jogging him*). *You* remember Mr Arnholm. Bolette's tutor.

WANGEL (*smiling*). You are a pair of . . . Well, it's only natural that you should . . . we should . . . as if she was still with us . . . But all the same.

He gives the bag to HILDE.

Put this in the surgery, would you, darling? No, I mean . . . girls . . . I don't . . . we shouldn't . . . every year . . . What will people say? There must be some other –

HILDE, *about to go by the garden gate with the bag, stops and points.*

HILDE. Look. Someone coming. It's Mr Arnholm.

BOLETTE (*looking*). Him? It can't be. Mr Arnholm? *That* old man?

WANGEL. Let me see, child. Good Lord, it is. It really is.

BOLETTE (*staring in amazement*). You're right. It is.

Enter ARNHOLM, *left down the road. He is wearing elegant morning clothes, with gold spectacles and uses a walking-cane. He seems somewhat edgy. He sees them, bows and comes through the gate.* WANGEL *goes to meet him.*

WANGEL. My dear Mr Arnholm, it's good to see you. Back in your old haunts. Welcome, welcome.

ARNHOLM. Doctor Wangel, thank you.

They shake hands and come up the garden together.

And these are the children.

He holds out his hands to them and looks at them.

I'd never have recognised them. Either of them.

WANGEL. Hardly surprising.

ARNHOLM. Well, Bolette perhaps. Yes. I'd have recognised Bolette.

WANGEL. What is it, eight, nine years? Lots of changes.

ARNHOLM (*looking round*). Not really. The trees are bigger . . . you've made an arbour *there* . . .

WANGEL. Small changes on the surface.

ARNHOLM. And naturally, two grown-up daughters now.

WANGEL. One, anyway.

HILDE (*sotto voce*). Father!

WANGEL. Let's sit in the shade. On the verandah. After you.

ARNHOLM. Thank you, Doctor, thank you.

They go up the steps. WANGEL *ushers* ARNHOLM *to the rocking-chair.*

WANGEL. Sit and rest. You look worn out. All that way!

ARNHOLM. Well, now that I'm here –

BOLETTE. Papa, shall we bring fruit-juice, soda-water? It's going to be hot.

WANGEL. Yes, please, girls. Fruit-juice, soda-water. And a drop of cognac.

BOLETTE. Cognac?

WANGEL. In case someone wants some.

BOLETTE. Hilde, you take Papa's bag to the surgery.

She goes in and closes the door. ARNHOLM *watches her leave.* HILDE *goes out, round the house, with the bag.*

ARNHOLM. What a fine young woman . . . what fine young women they are these days.

WANGEL (*sitting down*). You think so?

ARNHOLM. Bolette quite bowls me over. And Hilde too. But you, Doctor Wangel, how are you? Not thinking of moving?

WANGEL. It'll come, one day. I was born here, grew up here, I was happy here with . . . the Mrs Wangel who left us, the Mrs Wangel you knew when you were here.

ARNHOLM. Yes. Yes.

WANGEL. Now I'm happy with . . . the one who came
in her place. Fate's been good to me, good to me.

ARNHOLM. Have you children, the second Mrs Wangel?

WANGEL. A boy. Two, three years ago. We didn't keep
him long. When he was four or five months old, he
died.

ARNHOLM. And Mrs Wangel? She's not here today?

WANGEL. She will be, later. She's gone for a swim.
'Taking the waters.' She goes every day, this time of
year. Whatever the weather.

ARNHOLM. She's an invalid?

WANGEL. Not exactly. This last two years, there's been . . .
she's been . . . it's nothing serious. I can't put a name
to it. As if . . . as if getting into the sea was vital to
her, her life, her happiness . . .

ARNHOLM. She was always the same.

WANGEL (*with a light smile*). Of course, you knew her
before. When you were tutor out in Skjoldvik.

ARNHOLM. The pastor's children, yes. She often called.
And *I* saw *her*, when I called at the lighthouse to visit
her father.

WANGEL. Those old days made a deep impression on
her. People here don't understand. 'The mermaid.'
That's what they call her.

ARNHOLM. Really?

WANGEL. Talk to her about the old days. It'll help her.

ARNHOLM (*with a surprised look*). You think so?

WANGEL. I know so.

ELLIDA (*off, in the garden right*). Wangel. Wangel, is that you?

WANGEL (*getting up*). Here, darling.

Enter ELLIDA, *from among the trees on the foreshore. Her hair is wet, straggling over her shoulders, and she wears a large, light bathing-wrap.* ARNHOLM *gets up.*

WANGEL (*smiling and holding out his hands to her*). Here comes my mermaid now.

ELLIDA *hurries up the verandah steps and takes his hands.*

ELLIDA. Thank Heavens you're back. When did you arrive?

WANGEL. Just now. A few minutes ago.

He indicates ARNHOLM.

Now, say hello to an old friend . . .

ELLIDA (*shaking* ARNHOLM's *hand*). It's good to see you. Welcome. I'm sorry I wasn't –

ARNHOLM. Quite all right. No need to stand on ceremony . . .

WANGEL. Was it cold today?

ELLIDA. It's never cold. Stagnant, tepid. This far up the fjord, the sea is sick.

ARNHOLM. Sick?

ELLIDA. And if people swim in it, it makes them sick too.

WANGEL (*lightly*). Just what we need in a health resort.

ARNHOLM. My dear Mrs Wangel, I imagine that you understand the sea and its ways, better than anyone . . .

ELLIDA. Maybe so. Probably. Look how the girls have been decorating the place in your honour.

WANGEL (*embarrassed*). Hm.

He looks at his watch.

I'm afraid I have to –

ARNHOLM. *My* honour? Truly?

ELLIDA. You don't think we do this every day? Oof, it's stifling up here.

She goes down into the garden.

Come down here. At least there's a breath of a breeze.

She sits in the arbour. ARNHOLM *goes to her.*

ARNHOLM. Quite a gale, I'd say.

ELLIDA. Of course, you're used to Kristiania. Close, stuffy, they say it's unbearable in summer.

WANGEL (*who has also gone into the garden*). Ellida, darling, d'you mind if I leave you to look after Arnholm for a minute or two?

ELLIDA. You're busy?

WANGEL. Surgery. Then I have to change. I'll be as quick as I can.

ARNHOLM (*sitting down in the arbour*). Don't hurry on my account, old friend. Mrs Wangel and I will manage. We'll pass the time.

WANGEL (*nodding*). Of course you will. Till later, then.

Exit left through the garden. Pause.

ELLIDA. It's nice here. This arbour.

ARNHOLM. Very nice.

ELLIDA. *My* arbour. I had it made. Or rather, Doctor Wangel had it made, to please me.

ARNHOLM. You sit here often?

ELLIDA. Most of the time.

ARNHOLM. Sit here with the girls?

ELLIDA. They prefer the verandah.

ARNHOLM. And Doctor Wangel?

ELLIDA. He's in and out, up and down, here with me, up there with the children.

ARNHOLM. You prefer it that way?

ELLIDA. We all prefer it. Each in our own small corner. We can call to each other whenever we like, when we've anything to say.

ARNHOLM (*after a thoughtful pause*). The last time I met you . . . in Skjoldvik . . . years ago now . . .

ELLIDA. Ten years, at least.

ARNHOLM. At least. Out at the lighthouse. 'The heathen', that pastor called you. Because your father gave you the name of a ship, not a Christian human being –

ELLIDA. You said: 'The last time I met you' . . .

ARNHOLM. The last time, yes. I never imagined that next time I'd see you you'd be here, you'd be Mrs Wangel.

ELLIDA. In those days, Doctor Wangel wasn't . . . *She* was still alive, the children's first mother. Their real one.

ARNHOLM. Exactly. But even if he . . . if he'd had no obligations . . . I'd never have imagined . . .

ELLIDA. Ten years ago, neither would I.

ARNHOLM. I mean, Wangel! So kind, so generous, warm-hearted . . .

ELLIDA (*with warm sincerity*). He's a wonderful man.

ARNHOLM. But you . . . he . . . I mean, you're entirely different people.

ELLIDA. Entirely.

ARNHOLM. How ever did it happen? I mean, how did it happen?

ELLIDA. My dear Mr Arnholm, I can't explain. Don't ask me. Even if I could, you wouldn't understand.

ARNHOLM. Mm. (*More softly.*) Have you ever told him . . . your husband . . . ever mentioned me to him? I mean, the false step I once . . . I was once rash enough to . . .

ELLIDA. No. Good Heavens! How can you think I'd . . . ?

ARNHOLM. That's a relief. You've no idea . . . I was
embarrassed to think –

ELLIDA. All I've told him is that I was fond of you, that
you were my dearest and truest friend out there.

ARNHOLM. Thank you. But tell me: after I left, you
didn't write . . .

ELLIDA. I didn't want to hurt you. Hearing from
someone who . . . who couldn't do as you asked. It
would have been opening old wounds. I decided.

ARNHOLM. Perhaps you were right.

ELLIDA. And *you* never wrote to *me*.

ARNHOLM (*looking at her in mock reproach*). Me write first?
Pick myself up, start the whole thing off again?

ELLIDA. No. I see that. And since then . . . have you . . .
is there anyone else?

ARNHOLM. No one. I'm faithful to my memories.

ELLIDA (*half-mocking*). Forget them! Sad, old memories.
Set your sights on marriage, happiness.

ARNHOLM. And as soon as possible, Mrs Wangel. I'm
ashamed to admit it, but I'll soon be forty.

ELLIDA. Don't waste time, then. (*Seriously, quietly, after
a pause.*) Mr Arnholm . . . my dear . . . I'll tell you
now . . . I couldn't have told you then, if my life
depended on it.

ARNHOLM. What?

ELLIDA. Ten years ago, when you took that . . . false step you called it . . . I had to answer the way I did.

ARNHOLM. You'd nothing to offer but friendship. I understand.

ELLIDA. But you didn't know that my heart, my whole being, were somewhere else.

ARNHOLM. What, then?

ELLIDA. Yes, then.

ARNHOLM. You're wrong. It can't be. You and Wangel! You hadn't even met him.

ELLIDA. Not Wangel.

ARNHOLM. You mean . . . ten years ago . . . away out there, at Skjoldvik . . . ? I can't remember a single person there you could have had feelings for.

ELLIDA. You're right. It was . . . foolishness, madness.

ARNHOLM. Go on.

ELLIDA. I wasn't free, then. That's all you need to know.

ARNHOLM. And if you had been free?

ELLIDA. What d'you mean?

ARNHOLM. Would your answer have been different? To my letter, then?

ELLIDA. Who can tell? When Wangel came, it was different.

ARNHOLM. So why tell me what you've told me? Not free!

ELLIDA *gets up agitatedly.*

ELLIDA. Because I must confess to someone. No, don't get up.

ARNHOLM. Your husband doesn't know?

ELLIDA. Right from the start I told him I'd . . . my thoughts were . . . He's never wanted to know any more. We've never mentioned it. Madness, that's all it was, and it finished as soon as it started. In a sort of way.

ARNHOLM (*getting up*). A sort of way? Not completely?

ELLIDA. Yes! Completely! Arnholm, please, dear Arnholm, it's not what you think. I don't understand it. I can't explain it. If I tried to tell you, you'd think I was ill, insane.

ARNHOLM. My dear good woman, now you *have* to tell me.

ELLIDA. Ha, I'll try. But how could you, such a sensible man, ever understand –

She glances off, and stops.

Later. Someone's coming.

Enter LYNGSTRAND *down the road, left. He comes into the garden. He has a flower in his buttonhole and carries a bouquet wrapped in paper and tied with ribbon. He hesitates at the foot of the verandah steps.* ELLIDA *speaks from the arbour.*

ELLIDA. Mr Lyngstrand, are you looking for the girls?

LYNGSTRAND (*turning*). Mrs Wangel, I didn't see you there.

He goes closer.

Not the girls. You, Mrs Wangel. You invited me to pay a call one day, d'you remember?

ELLIDA. So I did. Well, how good to see you.

LYNGSTRAND. Thank you. Quite by chance, I heard that today's a special day for you all.

ELLIDA. You heard that?

LYNGSTRAND. So I made so bold . . . Mrs Wangel, these are for you.

He offers her the flowers. She smiles.

ELLIDA. For me? Mr Lyngstrand, shouldn't you be giving them to Mr Arnholm? Himself, in person? I mean, they are in his honour.

LYNGSTRAND (*looking at them both, baffled*). I'm sorry. I don't know this gentleman. I . . . these are for the birthday, Mrs Wangel.

ELLIDA. In that case, you *are* mistaken. No one here has a birthday today.

LYNGSTRAND (*smiling quietly*). I understand. I'd no idea it was a secret.

ELLIDA. What do you understand?

LYNGSTRAND. Happy Birthday, Mrs Wangel.

ELLIDA. Pardon?

ARNHOLM (*looking at her in surprise*). Today? It can't be. It isn't.

ELLIDA (*to* LYNGSTRAND). Whatever gave you that idea?

LYNGSTRAND. Well, I . . . young Miss Hilde. I looked in earlier, and asked the young ladies what all the flowers and flags were for.

ELLIDA. Yes?

LYNGSTRAND. And Miss Hilde said today was her mother's birthday.

ELLIDA. Her mother's . . . Ah.

ARNHOLM. Ah.

He and ELLIDA *look at one another: they see what's happened.*

Well, Mrs Wangel, if this young gentleman's found you out . . .

ELLIDA (*to* LYNGSTRAND). Since you've found me out . . .

LYNGSTRAND *once again offers her his flowers.*

LYNGSTRAND. Please . . . my very best wishes . . .

ELLIDA (*taking the flowers*). Mr Lyngstrand, thank you. Would you like to sit a moment?

The three of them sit in the arbour.

You must understand, Mr Lyngstrand: my birthday, no one was supposed to know.

ARNHOLM. No one outside the family.

ELLIDA (*putting the flowers on the table*). Exactly. Just the family.

LYNGSTRAND. On my honour, I won't tell a soul.

ELLIDA. No, it's all right. Tell me, how are you? You're looking a little better.

LYNGSTRAND. Making progress. At least I think so. And next year, if I can get to the Mediterranean . . .

ELLIDA. The girls said you were planning a trip.

LYNGSTRAND. One of my patrons, in Bergen, has offered to finance me. Next year.

ELLIDA. However did you find him?

LYNGSTRAND. It was amazing. I served on one of his ships.

ELLIDA. You liked the sea?

LYNGSTRAND. Not remotely. When my mother died, my father couldn't stand me hanging round the house. So he sent me to sea. On the voyage home, we were wrecked in the English Channel. As far as I was concerned, a stroke of luck.

ARNHOLM. You're joking.

LYNGSTRAND. No. That's where I got my . . . weakness. In the chest. The water was freezing, and I was in it for ages before they picked me up . . . After that, no more seafaring. A stroke of luck.

ARNHOLM. I still don't –

LYNGSTRAND. The weakness isn't serious. And now I can be a sculptor, fulfil my ambition. Imagine, soft clay, yielding clay, you're holding it, shaping it . . .

ELLIDA. Shaping what, exactly? Mermen and mermaids? Vikings?

LYNGSTRAND. Nothing like that. I'm planning . . . as soon as I'm fit enough . . . a big piece . . . a group, it's called.

ELLIDA. A group of what?

LYNGSTRAND. Something from my own experience.

ARNHOLM. Best stick to that.

ELLIDA. But what, exactly?

LYNGSTRAND. There'll be a woman, a sailor's wife, lying asleep, anxious, dreaming . . . I think I can make it clear she's dreaming.

ARNHOLM. Just the one figure?

LYNGSTRAND. No, two of them. The other one . . . a kind of *gestalt* . . . a manifestation . . . Her husband, he's been away, she's been unfaithful, and now he's drowned.

ARNHOLM. Good Heavens!

ELLIDA. You don't mean drowned.

LYNGSTRAND. Yes, drowned. At sea. And still he comes home. It's very mysterious. He stands there, beside the bed, and gazes at her. He's dripping wet, you know, like when they pull you out of the sea.

ELLIDA (*leaning back in the chair*). It's amazing. (*Closing her eyes.*) I can see it, every detail.

ARNHOLM. But for Heaven's sake, Mr . . . Mr . . . you said it was to be something from your own experience.

LYNGSTRAND. It is. Well, sort of.

ARNHOLM. You've seen a dead man come back to –

LYNGSTRAND. Of course not, not personally, not in so many . . . What I mean is –

ELLIDA (*eagerly*). Tell me everything about it. I want to know everything about it.

ARNHOLM (*lightly*). Of course you do. Just your thing: what with the sea, and everything.

ELLIDA. Tell us what happened, Mr Lyngstrand.

LYNGSTRAND. We were due to sail home, in the brig, from Halifax, Nova Scotia. We had to leave the second mate behind in hospital. So we took on an American in his place. The new second mate –

ELLIDA. The American?

LYNGSTRAND. Yes. Borrowed a pile of old newspapers from the captain one day, and never stopped reading them. Said he wanted to learn Norwegian.

ELLIDA. What happened?

LYNGSTRAND. One evening, it was filthy weather. All hands on deck, except the second mate and me. He'd sprained his ankle and couldn't walk on it; I was lying in my bunk, ill. There he was, sitting in the fo'c'sle, reading those confounded papers . . .

ELLIDA. Go on. Go on.

LYNGSTRAND. Suddenly – there he was, still sitting – I heard him give a a kind of roar. I looked at him; he was white as chalk. He took the paper and started crumpling it, tearing it to pieces – all in total silence.

ELLIDA. He didn't say a word?

LYNGSTRAND. Not right away. But then he said, as if to himself, 'Married. Another man. While I was away.'

ELLIDA (*half to herself, shutting her eyes*). *That's* what he said?

LYNGSTRAND. And in perfect Norwegian. He must have had a genius for languages, that man.

ELLIDA. Then . . . ? What happened next?

LYNGSTRAND. The oddest part of all. I'll never forget. He said, in the same quiet voice, 'She's still mine, and mine she'll always be. She'll go with me, even if I have to go back home and fetch her, like a drowned man from Davy Jones's locker.'

ELLIDA *pours a glass of water, her hand shaking.*

ELLIDA. Oof, it's close today.

LYNGSTRAND. He said it with such firmness, such willpower, I was sure he'd do it.

ELLIDA. D'you know . . . What happened to him afterwards?

LYNGSTRAND. Mrs Wangel, for sure, he's dead.

ELLIDA (*startled*). How d'you know?

LYNGSTRAND. We were wrecked soon afterwards in the Channel. I was in the lifeboat with the captain and five others. The mate was in the dinghy, with the American and one other man.

ELLIDA. And nothing's been heard of them since then?

LYNGSTRAND. Mrs Wangel, nothing. I had a letter from my patron the other day. He said so. That's why I want to make a group of it. They're in my mind's eye: the faithless wife, the avenger who still comes home even though he's drowned. I can imagine them exactly.

ELLIDA. So can I.

She gets up. LYNGSTRAND *politely rises with her.*

Let's go inside. No, let's find my husband. It's stifling here.

She comes out of the arbour.

LYNGSTRAND. I really should be going. I only called to say 'Happy Birthday'.

ELLIDA. If you really must go.

She shakes his hand.

Goodbye, and thanks for the flowers.

LYNGSTRAND *bows and exits left through the garden gate.* ARNHOLM *gets up and goes to* ELLIDA.

ARNHOLM. Mrs Wangel, my dear, you're quite upset.
This story –

ELLIDA. I suppose so. I –

ARNHOLM. After all, it's exactly what you must have
been expecting.

ELLIDA (*amazed*). Expecting?

ARNHOLM. It's obvious.

ELLIDA. You mean, he's coming back. Like . . . that?

ARNHOLM. For Heaven's sake, no. That's sculptor's
nonsense.

ELLIDA. Arnholm, dear friend, there may be something
in it.

ARNHOLM. The dead man? Is that what's upsetting
you? That nonsense? I thought –

ELLIDA. What?

ARNHOLM. I thought – well, obviously – that you were
upset because the family were celebrating without you
knowing, your husband and his children living
memories you could never share.

ELLIDA. It isn't that. I've no right to claim my husband
for myself alone.

ARNHOLM. I think you have.

ELLIDA. I haven't. And in any case, perhaps I have a life
they can't share.

ARNHOLM (*slowly*). Are you saying . . . are you telling
me . . . you don't love your husband?

ELLIDA. Of course I do. With all my heart. I came to love him. That's why it's so terrible, it's unbelievable, impossible –

ARNHOLM. Please tell me. Whatever's troubling you. Mrs Wangel, I insist.

ELLIDA. Dear friend, I can't. Not now. Later, perhaps.

BOLETTE *comes down the verandah steps into the garden.*

BOLETTE. Papa's finished surgery. Shall we sit inside, all of us?

ELLIDA. Yes, let's.

WANGEL, *who has changed his clothes, comes round the house with* HILDE.

WANGEL. There we are! All yours! D'you know what I fancy: a long, cool glass of something.

ELLIDA. I've something to show you.

She fetches the bouquet from the arbour.

HILDE. Aren't they pretty! Where did they come from?

ELLIDA. Lyngstrand the sculptor brought them, Hilde.

HILDE (*not expecting this*). Lyngstrand?

BOLETTE (*uneasily*). Has he come again again?

ELLIDA (*with a half-smile*). He came to bring these. A birthday bouquet. *You* know.

BOLETTE (*glancing at* HILDE). Ah . . .

HILDE (*muttered*). The pig.

WANGEL (*painfully embarrassed*). Hm. The thing is . . .
Darling Ellida . . . My dear, I must tell you –

ELLIDA (*interrupting him*). Come on, girls. Let's put them
in water with the others.

She goes up the steps on to the verandah.

BOLETTE (*aside to* HILDE). She's all *right*, you see?

HILDE (*aside, crossly*). Monkey-tricks. She's putting it on to
please Papa.

WANGEL, *on the verandah, presses* ELLIDA's *hand.*

WANGEL. Oh Ellida, thank you. What you've just done
. . . oh thank you.

ELLIDA (*arranging the flowers*). Don't be silly. Why shouldn't
I join in with the rest of you? After all, it's mother's
birthday.

ARNHOLM. Hm.

He goes to join WANGEL *and* ELLIDA. *The girls stay in
the garden.*

End of Act One.

ACT TWO

Up at the Viewpoint, a wooded hill behind the town. Towards the rear, landmark and weathervane. Round the landmark and in the foreground, large boulders used as seats. Rear, in the far distance below, the fjord with its islands and headlands. (Open sea not visible.) It is twilight on a clear summer evening, and the sky and distant mountains are bathed in orange glow. A group of voices singing folksongs can be heard from the lower slopes, down right.

Groups of YOUNG PEOPLE *from the town, men and women in pairs, walk up the path right, pass the landmark and exit left, making friendly conversation. After a pause enter* BALLESTED. *He is guiding a party of foreign tourists, and is hung round with the shawls and bags of the ladies. He gesures upwards with his stick.*

BALLESTED. *Sehen Sie, meine Herrschaften – dort* that way *liegt eine andere* height. *Das wollen wir besteigen* as well, *und so herunter. Mesdames, messieurs, vous voyez là-haut . . .*

He leads them off left, still talking. HILDE *hurries up the path right, stands and looks back. Pause, then* BOLETTE *comes up the same way.*

BOLETTE. Why on earth are we running away from Lyngstrand?

HILDE. Look at him crawling along. I can't bear to walk so slowly.

BOLETTE. You know he's an invalid.

HILDE. D'you think it's serious?

BOLETTE. Oh yes.

HILDE. He was at surgery this afternoon. I wonder what Papa thinks.

BOLETTE. A tumour in the lungs, Papa told me. Something like that. He hasn't long.

HILDE. I knew it.

BOLETTE. For Heaven's sake don't tell him.

HILDE. *I* know! (*Lower.*) It's a miracle he's crawled up this far. Poor old Hans. Don't you think he has to be a Hans?

BOLETTE (*whisper*). Behave yourself. I'm warning you!

Enter LYNGSTRAND *right. He is carrying a parasol.*

LYNGSTRAND. There you are. I'm sorry I couldn't keep up.

HILDE. Nice parasol.

LYNGSTRAND. It's your mother's. She said I could use it as a stick. I forgot my stick.

BOLETTE. Are they still down there? Papa and the others?

LYNGSTRAND. Your father went into the tearoom for a moment, and the others are sitting outside listening to the music. They'll be up in a minute, your mother said.

HILDE (*standing examining him*). You're tired now.

LYNGSTRAND. Just a bit. I think I'll sit down.

He sits on the stone downstage right. HILDE *stands and faces him.*

HILDE. D'you know there's going to be dancing, down by the bandstand?

LYNGSTRAND. So they were saying.

HILDE. D'you like dancing?

BOLETTE (*who is gathering flowers from among the heather*). Hilde, let Mr Lyngstrand catch his breath.

LYNGSTRAND (*to* HILDE). Yes, Miss Wangel, I'd love to dance, if I was able to.

HILDE. Hm. You don't know how to?

LYNGSTRAND. No. But that's not what I meant. I can't, because of my chest.

HILDE. You said it was weak.

LYNGSTRAND. That's right.

HILDE. It must really get you down.

LYNGSTRAND. Not particularly. (*With a smile.*) It makes everyone really kind and helpful.

HILDE. And of course it's nothing serious.

LYNGSTRAND. Not in the least. Or so your father told me.

HILDE. It'll sort itself when you go on holiday.

LYNGSTRAND. It'll sort itself.

BOLETTE (*with flowers*). Here, Mr Lyngstrand. Put this in your buttonhole.

LYNGSTRAND. Thanks, Miss Wangel. That's very kind of you.

HILDE (*looking off, right*). They're coming.

BOLETTE (*also looking*). I hope they don't miss the turning. Yes, they've gone the wrong way.

LYNGSTRAND (*getting up*). I'll run down and tell them.

HILDE. You'll have to shout.

BOLETTE. You'll wear yourself out again.

LYNGSTRAND. I'm all right going *down*.

Exit right.

HILDE. Oh yes, going down. (*Watching him.*) Look at him, jumping. He hasn't realised he'll have to come up again.

BOLETTE. Poor man.

HILDE. What if he proposed? Would you accept?

BOLETTE. Don't be silly.

HILDE. I mean, if he wasn't weak in the chest, if he wasn't going to die. *Then* would you accept him?

BOLETTE. No, *you* have him.

HILDE. I don't want him. He's penniless. Hardly supports himself.

BOLETTE. So why does he fascinate you so much?

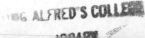

HILDE. Obviously: his 'weakness'.

BOLETTE. I've never noticed you being sorry for him.

HILDE. I'm not. It's *exciting* –

BOLETTE. What is?

HILDE. To look at him, make him say nothing's wrong with him, he's going abroad, he's going to be an artist. He's so sure, so happy. And all the time we know it won't happen. Any of it. He won't survive. It's *thrilling*.

BOLETTE. Thrilling.

HILDE. Yes, thrilling. If that's all right with you.

BOLETTE. You're a *horrid* child.

HILDE. Why shouldn't I be? If I want to? (*Gazing off.*) At last! Arnholm *hates* climbing. (*Turning.*) That reminds me: d'you know what I noticed about Arnholm when we were having dinner?

BOLETTE. What?

HILDE. He's going bald. Getting thin on top.

BOLETTE. He is not.

HILDE. And he's got wrinkly eyes. My God, Bolette, d'you remember how stuck on him you were when he was your tutor?

BOLETTE (*lightly*). Just imagine. I cried for a week once, just because he said Bolette was an ugly name.

HILDE. Just fancy. (*Looking off again.*) Look, there. She's taken his arm, the 'lady from the sea'. She's jabbering

away at him. Not to Papa. D'you think they're sweet
on each other?

BOLETTE. Hilde! How can you say such things about
her? We were getting on so much better, all of us.

HILDE. You think so? That's what you think? You're
wrong. We'll never get on well with that one. She
doesn't suit us, we don't suit her. What was Papa
thinking of, to drag her home? One of these days she'll
go mad on us. I'm telling you.

BOLETTE. Mad? Why should she?

HILDE. It's possible. Her mother did. Went mad and
died.

BOLETTE. You poke your nose into everything. Don't
mention it, that's all. For Papa's sake, behave yourself.
D'you hear me, Hilde?

Enter WANGEL, ELLIDA, ARNHOLM *and*
LYNGSTRAND, *right.*

ELLIDA (*pointing into the background*). It's away out there.

ARNHOLM. It must be.

ELLIDA. The open sea.

BOLETTE (*to* ARNHOLM). Isn't it pretty up here?

ARNHOLM. Magnificent! Look at the view.

WANGEL. You've never been up here before?

ARNHOLM. In my day, it was inaccessible. Not even a
footpath.

WANGEL. And certainly no gardens. This is all quite recent.

BOLETTE. Over that way, Pilot's Point, the view's even better.

WANGEL. D'you want to try, Ellida?

ELLIDA (*sitting on one of the stones, right*). No thanks. You go, the rest of you. I'll wait for you here.

WANGEL. I'll stay with you. The girls can take Mr Arnholm.

BOLETTE. Mr Arnholm, are you coming?

ARNHOLM. Oh yes. Is there a proper path?

BOLETTE. Absolutely.

HILDE. Wide enough for two to go arm-in-arm.

ARNHOLM (*lightly*). Is that so, Miss Hilde? Really? (*To* BOLETTE.) Shall we try it, see if she's right?

BOLETTE (*hiding a smile*). If you like. Why not?

Exeunt left, arm-in-arm.

HILDE (*to* LYNGSTRAND). Shall we go too?

LYNGSTRAND. Arm-in-arm?

HILDE. Yes, if you like.

He takes her arm, and laughs with pleasure.

LYNGSTRAND. I say! I say!

HILDE. What d'you say?

LYNGSTRAND. People will think we're engaged.

HILDE. Mr Lyngstrand, is this the first time you've taken a lady's arm?

Exeunt left.

WANGEL (*standing at rear by the landmark*). Ellida, darling, at last a moment to ourselves.

ELLIDA. Sit here by me.

WANGEL (*sitting*). It's relaxed here. Still. It's time for us to talk.

ELLIDA. What about?

WANGEL. Ellida, you. The two of us. I don't think we can go on like this.

ELLIDA. What is it you want?

WANGEL. Trust. Absolute trust. To be the way we were.

ELLIDA. Oh, so do I. But it's impossible.

WANGEL. I think I understand. Things you've said, little things . . . I think I understand.

ELLIDA (*with force*). You don't. Don't say that.

WANGEL. I do. Ellida, you're an open, honest person . . . loyal –

ELLIDA. Yes.

WANGEL. If you're to be happy in a relationship, it must be a hundred per cent, entire.

ELLIDA (*looking at him in alarm*). What d'you mean?

WANGEL. A second wife. You just weren't made for it.

ELLIDA. Why d'you say this now?

WANGEL. I wondered, before. But today I saw it, clearly. The girls' celebration: you thought I was part of that. Well. Memories, we can't wipe them out. Not mine, anyway. I . . . I can't.

ELLIDA. My dear, I know.

WANGEL. But you don't understand. You think their mother's still alive for me . . . a kind of unseen presence, always with us. You think I split my heart in two, half hers, half yours. That's what you think, and you can't bear it. You think it's, I don't know, immoral, and that's why you can't – won't – go on as we were, husband, wife, the way we were.

ELLIDA (*getting up*). Is that what you see, Edvard? See clearly?

WANGEL. Today, yes, clearly: the whole thing, entirely.

ELLIDA. The whole thing. You can't, you mustn't . . .

WANGEL (*getting up*). Ellida, darling, I know all the rest of it.

ELLIDA (*anxiously*). You know?

WANGEL. Of course. You can't bear this place. The mountains get you down, close in on you. There's not enough light, the horizon's cramped, the air's not pure enough, not healthy enough.

ELLIDA. That's right. Light, dark, summer, winter, it haunts me, I'm homesick, I long for it, the sea.

WANGEL. Darling, I know.

He lays his hand on her head.

Poor child, sick child . . . You must go home.

ELLIDA. What d'you mean?

WANGEL. Literally: go home. We'll move.

ELLIDA. Move?

WANGEL. Somewhere out beside the sea, the open sea. Where you can find a home, the home you long for.

ELLIDA. Edvard, we can't. It's impossible. How could you be happy, anywhere but here?

WANGEL. And how d'you think I could be happy here, without you?

ELLIDA. I'm not going away. I'm here. I'm yours.

WANGEL. Ellida, are you?

ELLIDA. Don't talk about moving. Your life is here, your heart and soul are here. All you do, all you stand for, here.

WANGEL. Well, even so, I think we should move, somewhere further out, beside the sea. I've made up my mind, Ellida.

ELLIDA. But what will we *gain* by it?

WANGEL. Your health, your peace of mind.

ELLIDA. I don't think so. And what about you? Never mind me: what will *you* gain by it?

WANGEL. You, darling.

ELLIDA. But you don't understand, you can't! It's impossible, unthinkable . . .

WANGEL. We'll find out. If your thoughts torment you here, the best thing to do is get you away, as far away as possible. And as soon as possible. I've made up my mind, I'm telling you.

ELLIDA. No! Let me tell you, in Heaven's name, tell you what's the matter.

WANGEL. Tell me. Tell me.

ELLIDA. You mustn't make yourself miserable for my sake. Especially when it won't help either of us.

WANGEL. What is it? Tell me the truth: exactly.

ELLIDA. As well as I can. As much as I understand. Sit here, beside me.

They sit on the stones.

WANGEL. Now, Ellida? Well?

ELLIDA. D'you remember the day you came out there and asked me if I could, if I would, be yours? How openly and honestly you talked about your first marriage? How happy it was, you said?

WANGEL. It was.

ELLIDA. Edvard, of course. That's not what I meant. But remember: on my side, I was just as honest with you. I said, frankly, that I'd had a previous relationship . . . a kind of engagement.

WANGEL. Kind of . . . ?

ELLIDA. Well, it was short, very short. He went away; I broke it off. I told you all this.

WANGEL. Ellida, my dear, why are you bringing this up again? It was none of my business. It is none of my business. I've never even asked you his name.

ELLIDA. You always try not to hurt me.

WANGEL (*smiling*). In any case, it's obvious who he was.

ELLIDA. What d'you mean?

WANGEL. Out there, Skjoldvik and round about, there weren't very many to choose from. In fact, there was really only one.

ELLIDA. You think it was Arnholm.

WANGEL. Wasn't it?

ELLIDA. No.

WANGEL. In that case, I'm baffled.

ELLIDA. D'you remember at the end of the year, that autumn, a big American ship docked in Skjoldvik for repairs?

WANGEL – and the captain was found murdered in his cabin one morning. I did the post-mortem.

ELLIDA. That's right.

WANGEL. The second mate was supposed to have done it.

ELLIDA. No one can prove it. He wasn't arrested.

WANGEL. No, but it's highly likely. Why else would he drown himself?

ELLIDA. He didn't drown himself. He escaped, on a ship going north.

WANGEL (*astonished*). How on earth d'you know that?

ELLIDA (*with difficulty*). Because . . . that second mate . . . he was the man I was engaged to.

WANGEL (*jumping up*). What? You're joking.

ELLIDA. No. He was the man.

WANGEL. In God's name, Ellida, how could you? Engage yourself to a . . . to a man like that, a total stranger? You don't even know his name.

ELLIDA. He said his name was Friman. Then. Later, when he wrote, he called himself Alfred Johnston.

WANGEL. Where was he from?

ELIDA. Finnmark. Or so he said. He was born in Finland, crossed the border when he was still a child. With his father, I think he said.

WANGEL. Finnish nationality.

ELLIDA. I think so.

WANGEL. Did you know anything else about him?

ELLIDA. Just that he was a boy when he went to sea. And that he'd travelled everywhere.

WANGEL. Nothing else?

ELLIDA. That's not what we talked about.

WANGEL. What did you talk about?

ELLIDA. Mainly, the sea.

WANGEL. How d'you mean, the sea?

ELLIDA. Storms, calm weather . . . Darkness at sea . . .
    Sun glinting on the waves . . . Whales, most of all,
    dolphins, seals basking on rocks in the morning sun . . .
    Gulls, sea-eagles, all kinds of sea-birds . . . The
    amazing thing is, when we talked about that kind
    of thing, I felt he was one of them, belonged to them,
    a sea-bird, a creature of the sea . . .

WANGEL. What about you?

ELLIDA. Oh, I belonged to them too.

WANGEL. That's why you said you'd marry him?

ELLIDA. He said I had to.

WANGEL. Had to? You'd no will of your own?

ELLIDA. Not when he was there. Afterwards, it all
    seemed strange.

WANGEL. Did you spend much time with him?

ELLIDA. No. He paid us a visit. At the lighthouse. That's
    how I met him. We saw each other a few times
    afterwards. But then there was that business with the
    captain. He had to leave.

WANGEL. Tell me about that.

ELLIDA. He sent me a note. Early in the morning, it was still dark. I was to meet him at Bratthammer: you know, the headland between Skjoldvik and the lighthouse.

WANGEL. I know where you mean.

ELLIDA. He said I should hurry. He had something to say to me.

WANGEL. And you went?

ELLIDA. I felt I'd no choice. When I got there, he told me he'd stabbed the captain during the night.

WANGEL. A confession!

ELLIDA. He said he'd had no choice. Justice demanded –.

WANGEL. Justice for what?

ELLIDA. He wouldn't tell me. It wasn't for me to hear, he said.

WANGEL. He said all this, no proof, and you believed him?

ELLIDA. It never occurred to me not to. In any case, he was leaving. And just as we were saying goodbye . . . you can't imagine what he did.

WANGEL. No, tell me!

ELLIDA. He took his key-ring out of his pocket. He had a ring on his finger. He took it off, and asked me for a little ring I wore. He put the two rings on the key-ring and said that the two of us were to be united to the sea.

WANGEL. United?

ELLIDA. That's what he said. Then he threw the key-ring and the rings into the sea, as far as he could.

WANGEL. Ellida, you went along with this . . . ?

ELLIDA. What could I do to stop it? I felt it *had* to happen. Next thing, God be thanked, he sailed.

WANGEL. And when he was gone?

ELLIDA. Oh, then I realised how silly and pointless the whole thing had been.

WANGEL. You mentioned letters. He wrote you letters?

ELLIDA. A line or two, from Archangel. He said he was crossing to America, gave me an address to write to.

WANGEL. And did you?

ELLIDA. Right away. I said everything was finished between us. He was never to think of me again, and I would never think of him.

WANGEL. And still he wrote again?

ELLIDA. Oh yes.

WANGEL. After what you said? What did he answer?

ELLIDA. He didn't even mention it. Wrote as if I'd never ended it between us. Said he'd let me know when he was ready, and I was to come at once.

WANGEL. Refused to let you go?

ELLIDA. I wrote again, almost word for word the first letter, but sharper.

WANGEL. That made him agree?

ELLIDA. Not in the least. He wrote as calmly as before. Not a word about my breaking it off. I saw it was pointless, so I never wrote again.

WANGEL. Did you hear from him again?

ELLIDA. Three times. Once from California, once from China, and then from Australia. He said he was going to the gold-fields; that's the last I heard of him.

WANGEL. Ellida, that man had amazing power over you.

ELLIDA. It was terrifying.

WANGEL. But now you should forget him. Promise me, Ellida, my dear, my darling. We'll find another cure for you: fresh, sea air, salt air, none of this stuffy inland atmosphere. What d'you say?

ELLIDA. Don't say that! Don't think about it. What good will it do? It'll be the same there, just the same there. I'll never be rid of it.

WANGEL. Rid of what, Ellida?

ELLIDA. The way he controls me. His power, no one can imagine –

WANGEL. But you *are* rid of it. Years ago. You broke it off. It's over, in the past, forgotten.

ELLIDA (*jumping up*). That's the whole point. It isn't.

WANGEL. Not over.

ELLIDA. No, Edvard. And it never will be. Ever.

WANGEL (*in a choked voice*). Are you saying that all this time, in your heart of hearts, you've never been able to forget that stranger?

ELLIDA. I had forgotten him. But then it was as if he came again.

WANGEL. When?

ELLIDA. Three years ago. A little longer. When I was expecting the baby.

WANGEL. *Then?* Ellida, ah. I'm beginning to understand.

ELLIDA. My dear, how can you? What's come over me: no one will ever understand.

WANGEL (*looks at her, hurt*). I can't believe it. For three years now, you've given your heart to another man. Not to me, to another man.

ELLIDA. You're wrong. I love no one else but you.

WANGEL (*low*). Why then, in all that time, have you refused to . . . never agreed to . . . ?

ELLIDA. Because I was frightened. The stranger frightened me.

WANGEL. Frightened?

ELLIDA. So frightened. It comes from the sea, comes only from the sea. Edvard, I tell you –

The YOUNG PEOPLE *from the town pass by, bowing as they go. In the group are* ARNHOLM, BOLETTE, HILDE *and* LYNGSTRAND.

BOLETTE (*as they pass*). Are the two of you still here?

WILLDA. It's cooler here.

ARNHOLM. We're going down for a dance.

WANGEL. We won't be long.

HILDE. See you later.

ELLIDA. Mr Lyngstrand . . . A moment.

> LYNGSTRAND *waits*. ARNHOLM, HILDE *and*
> BOLETTE *go out, right*.

Will you be dancing?

LYNGSTRAND. Afraid not, Mrs Wangel.

ELLIDA. Best look after yourself. Your weak chest . . .
you're not quite better.

LYNGSTRAND. No.

ELLIDA (*hesitantly*). How long is it since you . . . made
that voyage?

LYNGSTRAND. When I was injured?

ELLIDA. The one you told us about this morning.

LYNGSTRAND. It was . . . I don't know . . . two, three
years ago.

ELLIDA. Three years?

LYNGSTRAND. More or less. We left America in
February. We were shipwrecked in March. The
equinoctial gales.

ELLIDA (*looking at* WANGEL). Exactly the time when –

WANGEL. My dear Ellida . . .

ELLIDA. Don't wait for us, Mr Lyngstrand. Go on ahead. But remember: no dancing!

LYNGSTRAND. I'll remember.

Exit, right.

WANGEL. Darling, why did you ask about that voyage?

ELLIDA. Johnston was on that ship. I'm certain.

WANGEL. What makes you think so?

ELLIDA (*not answering*). He discovered, on that voyage, that I'd married someone else. While he was away. And *that's* when, that's the exact moment when, all this came over me.

WANGEL. When you began being frightened?

ELLIDA. D'you know, sometimes, out of nowhere, I see him standing in front of me. Just to one side. He never faces me directly. Never speaks.

WANGEL. How does he look?

ELLIDA. Exactly the way he was, when I saw him last.

WANGEL. Ten years ago?

ELLIDA. At Bratthammer. He had an ornamental tiepin. That's how I know it's him. A pearl tiepin, a big, blue-white pearl like a fish's eye. A dead fish, glaring at me.

WANGEL. For Heaven's sake! Ellida, you're worse than I imagined. Worse than even *you* imagined.

ELLIDA. Help me. If you can. It's coming closer, closer.

WANGEL. You've been in this state for three whole years. Three years, and you never told me.

ELLIDA. How could I? Not till now, when I had to, for your sake. If I'd told you before, I'd have had to tell you the other thing, the unspeakable thing.

WANGEL. What unspeakable thing?

ELLIDA (*avoiding it*). It's all right. Don't ask me. My dear, just one more mystery. The eyes, how can we explain the baby's eyes?

WANGEL. My dear Ellida, I keep telling you it was all in your mind. The baby had exactly the same kind of eyes as any normal child.

ELLIDA. He didn't. Didn't you notice? His eyes changed colour with the sea. When the fjord was calm and sunny, so were his eyes. When it was stormy . . . I saw, I saw, even if you didn't.

WANGEL (*humouring her*). Well, if you say so. But what about it? Why does it matter?

ELLIDA (*softly, going nearer*). I saw eyes like that before.

WANGEL. When? Where?

ELLIDA. Ten years ago. At Bratthammer.

WANGEL (*startled*). God in Heaven.

ELLIDA (*in a low voice, trembling*). My child had the stranger's eyes.

WANGEL (*an involuntary shout*). Ellida!

ELLIDA, *in despair, clasps her hands over her head.*

ELLIDA. *Now* do you understand why I won't . . . I can't . . . I *daren't* . . . any more with you?

She turns and runs down the hill right. WANGEL *plunges after her.*

WANGEL. Ellida! Oh Ellida! Darling!

End of Act Two.

ACT THREE

A corner of WANGEL's *garden, beside a pond, right. It is remote, dark, damp, overshadowed by ancient trees. A fence lies between it and the path and fjord beyond. Far in the distance, across the fjord, mountains rising to high peaks.*

Late afternoon, just before twilight. BOLETTE *is sitting sewing on a stone seat. Beside her are a couple of books and her sewing basket.* HILDE *and* LYNGSTRAND *are standing together, fishing in the pond.*

HILDE. Shh! There's a whopper, there!

She points. He looks.

LYNGSTRAND. Where?

HILDE (*pointing*). Down there. There's another one! Another!

She glances off, through the trees.

Damn! Now *he's* coming. He'll scare them.

BOLETTE (*looking up*). Who's coming?

HILDE. Your tutor, missie.

BOLETTE. My tutor?

HILDE. Well, he certainly isn't *mine*!

Enter ARNHOLM, *right from among the trees.*

ARNHOLM. Are there still fish in there?

HILDE. A few aged goldfish.

ARNHOLM. Those goldfish still living?

HILDE. Tough as old boots. But today we're polishing
   some of them off.

ARNHOLM. You should try your luck in the fjord.

LYNGSTRAND. We prefer the pond. More . . .
   mysterious.

HILDE. More exciting. Have you been swimming?

ARNHOLM. Oh yes. I've just been changing.

HILDE. I hope you didn't go out of your depth.

ARNHOLM. I'm no great swimmer.

HILDE. Can you do backstroke?

ARNHOLM. No.

HILDE. I can. (*To* LYNGSTRAND.) Let's try our luck on
   the other side.

   HILDE *and* LYNGSTRAND *go out round the pond, right.*
   ARNHOLM *goes to* BOLETTE.

ARNHOLM. Miss Wangel . . . Bolette, sitting here by
   yourself?

BOLETTE. I often do.

ARNHOLM. Your mother not here?

BOLETTE. She and Papa went out for a walk.

ARNHOLM. How is she this afternoon?

BOLETTE. Not sure. I forgot to ask her.

ARNHOLM. What are you reading?

BOLETTE. This one's botany, this one's geography.

ARNHOLM. Still studying?

BOLETTE. When I've time. I mean, from the housekeeping.

ARNHOLM. Doesn't your mother – your stepmother – help you with that?

BOLETTE. I see to it all. I did it for two years, after Papa was widowed. I've gone on doing it.

ARNHOLM. But you'd still rather study.

BOLETTE. As much as I can. To find out about the world. Down here, we're completely cut off. Or almost.

ARNHOLM. My dear Bolette, you're joking.

BOLETTE. We're like the goldfish in the pond. They have the fjord just next door, with shoals of wild fish swmming in and out. And they've no idea. They're tame, poor things, they don't know what freedom *is*.

ARNHOLM. I don't think they'd like it, if they broke out there.

BOLETTE. If they had their chance, they still might take it.

ARNHOLM. In any case, you're not cut off. In summer, anyway. This place is a crossroads, a gathering-point, a Mecca for passers-by.

BOLETTE (*lightly*). That's right: make fun of us. You're a passer-by yourself.

ARNHOLM. Make fun . . . ? What makes you think so?

BOLETTE. 'A crossroads, a Mecca' – that's the nonsense they talk in town. They're always saying it.

ARNHOLM. True enough.

BOLETTE. There isn't a word of truth in it. Not if you live here all year round. The whole world streams through on its way to see the midnight sun – how does that affect us? *We* don't stream, *we* have no midnight sun. We're goldfish, goldfish in a pond.

ARNHOLM *sits beside her.*

ARNHOLM. Bolette, tell me a little: if you had anything you wanted, if someone granted you three wishes –

BOLETTE. They won't.

ARNHOLM. But if they did? What would you choose?

BOLETTE. First, to get away.

ARNHOLM. Before anything else?

BOLETTE. Yes. And second, to study a little more, learn more about everything.

ARNHOLM. When I was your tutor, your father was always saying he wanted you to go to university.

BOLETTE. Poor Papa. Always promising . . . but when it comes down to it . . . not one of life's *doers* . . .

ARNHOLM. I know what you mean. But haven't you told him all this? Shown him how you feel?

BOLETTE. I suppose not. No.

ARNHOLM. Don't you think you should? And soon, Bolette, before it's too late? Why don't you?

BOLETTE. Perhaps I'm not one of life's doers either: just like Papa.

ARNHOLM. Not true.

BOLETTE. Oh yes. In any case, Papa hasn't time to think about me and my future. He doesn't want to. Decisions like that, he puts them off as long as possible. And then there's Ellida.

ARNHOLM. Pardon?

BOLETTE. Papa and my stepmother . . . (*Correcting herself.*) Father and Mother don't *need* anyone else.

ARNHOLM. All the more reason for you to get away.

BOLETTE. It wouldn't be right. To abandon Papa.

ARNHOLM. My dear Bolette, it has to happen one day. So why not sooner than later?

BOLETTE. I suppose so. I ought to think of my future. Look for a position. When Papa . . . when he's gone, I'll have nothing to support me. But poor Papa, I'm afraid if I leave him.

ARNHOLM. Afraid?

BOLETTE. Of what'll become of him.

ARNHOLM. For Heaven's sake, there's your stepmother. *She's* here.

BOLETTE. She doesn't cope the way Mama did. Lots of things, important things: she doesn't *see* them, or chooses *not* to see them, or won't get involved . . . I don't know which it is.

ARNHOLM. I see what you mean.

BOLETTE. Papa's little ways. You must have noticed. He hasn't enough work, he has too much leisure, and she's no idea how to help him. Mind you, that's partly his own fault.

ARNHOLM. What d'you mean?

BOLETTE. Papa likes to be surrounded by smiling faces. Says the house should be full of sunshine and contentment. And I think, I wonder if he doesn't let her take things, medicines, that can't in the end be good for her.

ARNHOLM. You don't mean that.

BOLETTE. I can't put it out of my mind. She's so strange sometimes. (*With force.*) Why *should* I have to stay here? It isn't fair. I'm no use to Papa, and I *owe* it to myself . . . Don't I?

ARNHOLM. My dear Bolette, listen to me. We must take this further.

BOLETTE. What's the point? I think I was born to sit here by the goldfish-pond.

ARNHOLM. Of course you weren't. It's in your own hands.

BOLETTE (*hopefully*). You think so?

ARNHOLM. It's up to you entirely.

BOLETTE. Oh, if . . . ! If *you* spoke to Papa . . .

ARNHOLM. I intend to. But first, dear Bolette, I want to say something to you, with all my heart, with all my soul.

He glances left.

Ssh! Pretend nothing's happened. We'll talk about it later.

Enter ELLIDA, *left. She is hatless, but has a shawl over her head and shoulders. She is nervy.*

ELLIDA. What a beautiful evening. How nice it is out here.

ARNHOLM (*getting up*). Have you been for a walk?

ELLIDA. A long walk with Dr Wangel. Now we're going sailing.

BOLETTE. D'you want to sit a moment?

ELLIDA. No thanks. I couldn't.

BOLETTE (*moving along the seat*). There's plenty of room.

ELLIDA (*pacing about*). No, I can't. I couldn't.

ARNHOLM. Your walk's done you good. Put colour in your cheeks.

ELLIDA. I feel so . . . well, happy. Wonderfully happy. Safe, I feel so safe.

She looks out left.

What's that ship arriving?

BOLETTE *gets up to look.*

BOLETTE. The tour-boat from England.

ARNHOLM. They're mooring it. Does it always stop here?

BOLETTE. Just for half an hour. Then it goes on up the fjord.

ELLIDA. Then out again, tomorrow. To the open sea, the wide, free sea. Imagine going with it! If only . . .

ARNHOLM. Have you never been on the sea, Mrs Wangel?

ELLIDA. Short trips on the fjord, that's all.

BOLETTE (*sighing*). Dry land is all we have.

ARNHOLM. Our natural element.

ELLIDA. I don't think it's that at all.

ARNHOLM. You don't?

ELLIDA. I think that if the first human beings had made themselves used to living on the sea – in the sea, even – we'd have been far *better* than we are now. More successful, happier . . .

ARNHOLM. You really think so?

ELLIDA. It's possible. I've talked of it, often, with Dr Wangel.

ARNHOLM. And he – ?

ELLIDA. He agreed it was possible.

ARNHOLM (*lightly*). Oh, possible, I grant you. But now it's too late. We made the wrong decision all those years ago, and we're land creatures now, not sea creatures. Like it or not, the die is cast: there's no going back.

ELLIDA. Unfortunately. I think the whole human race knows it and regrets it: it's a hidden sorrow, and it's why our species is so miserable, deep down. I'm sure it is.

ARNHOLM. Dear Mrs Wangel, I haven't noticed we're miserable. Deep down. I think most people are happy, enjoy their lives – even if we don't know it, contentment's there like a deep, calm pool.

ELLIDA. You're wrong. Contentment's like autumn sunshine. Shadowed by the dark to come. Hints of sadness shadow human happiness, the way clouds drive across the fjord. One minute calm and bright, then without any warning –

BOLETTE. Don't think such gloomy thoughts. A moment ago you were cheerful, happy . . .

ELLIDA. That's right. It's ridiculous.

She glances anxiously about.

What's happened to your father? He said he'd meet me here. He promised. Where is he? He's forgotten. Mr Arnholm, please, will you look for him?

ARNHOLM. With pleasure.

ELLIDA. Tell him to hurry. Tell him I can't *see* him –

ARNHOLM. What d'you mean, can't see him?

ELLIDA. No, I mean, when he isn't with me, I sometimes forget what he looks like. As if I'd lost him. It's unbearable. Go on, go on!

She goes distractedly towards the pond.

BOLETTE (*to* ARNHOLM). I'll go with you. You don't –

ARNHOLM. It's all right. I'll –

BOLETTE (*in a low voice*). You don't understand. I'm worried. I'm afraid he's on the tour-boat.

ARNHOLM. Afraid?

BOLETTE. He goes to see if there's anyone he knows. And there's a bar on board . . .

ARNHOLM. Come on, then.

Exeunt left. ELLIDA *stands looking into the pond, murmuring to herself from time to time. Out on the footpath, the other side of the fence, a* STRANGER *appears left. He has bushy red hair and a beard, wears walking clothes and a cap and carries a haversack over one shoulder. He walks along the path, looking over the fence into the garden. When he sees* ELLIDA, *he gazes at her long and searchingly. Then he says, in a quiet voice:*

STRANGER. Ellida. Good evening.

ELLIDA *turns and cries*:

ELLIDA. Darling, you've come at last.

STRANGER. That's right: at last.

ELLIDA *stares at him, surprised and anxious.*

ELLIDA. A stranger. Who are you? You want someone here?

STRANGER. Ellida, you know the answer.

ELLIDA (*recoiling*). You know my name. Who is it you've come for?

STRANGER. You know it's you.

ELLIDA *draws back with a scream, takes a few paces backwards, her eyes fixed on him, then blurts out in a half-choked voice*:

ELLIDA. Your eyes. Your eyes.

STRANGER. Now you know who I am? I recognised you at once, Ellida.

ELLIDA. Don't look at me. Your eyes. I'll shout for help.

STRANGER. It's all right. You're safe. Ellida . . . I'm not here to hurt you.

ELLIDA (*hiding her eyes*). Don't look at me.

The STRANGER *leans on the fence.*

STRANGER. I came on the tour-boat.

ELLIDA (*looking at him, terrified*). What d'you want of me?

STRANGER. I promised: as soon as I could, I'd come.

ELLIDA. Go back. Go away. I wrote to you, I told you it was finished. There was nothing more. I told you.

STRANGER (*as if she'd never spoken*). I'd have come sooner, but I couldn't. Then it was possible, and here I am. Ellida.

ELLIDA. What d'you want from me? What are you thinking of? What have you come for?

STRANGER. You know perfectly well, Ellida: to fetch you.

ELLIDA (*shrinking away*). Fetch me? You can't. I –

STRANGER. What?

ELLIDA. You know I'm married.

STRANGER. Of course I know.

ELLIDA. And still . . . in spite of that you . . . you come to fetch me . . .

STRANGER. Exactly.

ELLIDA (*pressing her hands to her head*). It's unbearable. I can't . . . Unbearable.

STRANGER. You don't want to come?

ELLIDA (*hysterical*). Don't look at me.

STRANGER. I said: you don't want to come?

ELLIDA. No, no, no! I won't. Not ever. I won't. I can't, I won't. (*Lower.*) I daren't.

The STRANGER *climbs over the fence into the garden.*

STRANGER. Very well, Ellida. Let me say one thing, and then I'll leave you.

ELLIDA *tries to escape, but can't. She stands as if paralysed with terror, supporting herself on a tree beside the pond.*

ELLIDA. Don't touch me. Stay away. Don't come near me. Please don't touch me.

The STRANGER *goes a step or two towards her.*

STRANGER (*gently*). Ellida, you've no need to be afraid of me.

ELLIDA (*covering her eyes*). Don't look at me!

STRANGER. Don't be afraid. Don't be afraid.

WANGEL *comes through the garden. He speaks before he sees them.*

WANGEL. I'm sorry I kept you waiting.

ELLIDA *runs to him and clings to his arm.*

ELLIDA. Help me. Save me. If you can, oh save me.

WANGEL. Ellida, what on earth – ?

ELLIDA. Can't you see him? There, there!

WANGEL (*looking at the* STRANGER). What, this man?

He advances on the STRANGER.

Excuse me, who are you? And why are you in my garden?

STRANGER (*indicating* ELLIDA). My business is with *her*.

WANGEL. Is it indeed? So it was you who . . . (*To* ELLIDA.) They told me at the house, a stranger had called to see you.

STRANGER. That's right. *I* did.

WANGEL. You've business with my wife? (*Turning.*) Ellida, d'you know this man?

ELLIDA (*quietly, wringing her hands*). Oh I know him. I know him, yes.

WANGEL (*curtly*). *Well?*

ELLIDA. It's him. The man I . . . the man who . . .

WANGEL. Ah. Really. (*To the* STRANGER.) So you're Johnston?

STRANGER. Call me Johnston, if you want to. It isn't my name.

WANGEL. Oh, it isn't?

STRANGER. Not any longer.

WANGEL. And why are you bothering my wife? You've known all along that the lighthouse-keeper's daughter got married. And you know who to.

STRANGER. I found that out three years ago.

ELLIDA (*intrigued*). You found out – how?

STRANGER. I was coming home. To you, Ellida. I read it in the paper. An old paper, the local paper. Your wedding-announcement.

ELLIDA (*staring ahead*). But that's what –

STRANGER. I was surprised, Ellida. That business with the rings: that was a marriage, too.

ELLIDA (*hiding her face in her hands*). Aaah –

WANGEL. How dare you?

STRANGER. Had you forgotten?

ELLIDA (*as if his look forces it out of her*). Don't look at me!

WANGEL (*squaring up to him*). Deal with me, if you please, not her. This is very simple. You've discovered how things are; what point in staying? Why did you come and pester my wife in the first place?

STRANGER. I promised, as soon as I could, I'd fetch her.

WANGEL. Ellida! You said –

STRANGER. And Ellida promised, on her honour, to be waiting for me.

WANGEL. Mrs Wangel to you. Who said you could call my wife Ellida?

STRANGER. She belongs to me.

WANGEL. Belongs?

ELLIDA (*hiding behind him*). He'll never set me free.

WANGEL. How d'you make that out? *Belongs* to you?

STRANGER. She's told you about the rings? My ring, Ellida's ring?

WANGEL. Of course she has. And what about it? She ended it very soon afterwards. You got her letters, you know the situation exactly.

STRANGER. Ellida and I promised, equally, that the linking of the rings was as valid, as binding, as a wedding.

ELLIDA. I don't *want* it! I want nothing to do with you. Don't look at me. I don't, I won't.

WANGEL. If you think you can turn up here and make claims on her, because of a piece of childish nonsense, you're mad.

STRANGER. Oh yes. In the way you mean, I've no claim on her. I admit it.

WANGEL. So what are you here for? You don't imagine I'd let you kidnap her, abduct her against her will?

STRANGER. What good would that do? If Ellida comes with me, she must come of her own free will.

ELLIDA (*startled cry*). Free will!

WANGEL. You really imagine . . .

ELLIDA (*to herself*). My own free will.

WANGEL. You're out of your mind. Clear off. We've nothing more to do with you.

STRANGER (*looking at his watch*). I have to go on board.

He takes a step forward.

Ellida, I've done what I came to do.

Another step.

I've kept my promise.

ELLIDA (*shrinking back*). Don't touch me.

STRANGER. You can have till this time tomorrow to think it over.

WANGEL. What are you talking about? Clear off!

STRANGER (*ignoring him; to* ELLIDA). I'm going up the fjord with the tour-boat. I'll be back tomorrow evening. Ellida, I'll see you then. Wait for me here in the garden. And I prefer to settle this with no one else here, just you alone.

ELLIDA (*in a low voice, trembling, to* WANGEL). D'you hear what he's saying?

WANGEL. Don't be afraid. We'll find a way. We'll stop him.

STRANGER. Ellida, till tomorrow.

ELLIDA (*begging*). No, no. Tomorrow, no. Not ever.

STRANGER. If in the meantime you decide to come with me, far across the sea . . .

ELLIDA. Don't look at me.

STRANGER. All I mean is: if that's what you decide, be ready to leave.

WANGEL. Ellida, go inside.

ELLIDA. I can't. Help me. Save me.

STRANGER. Be clear on one thing: if you don't come with me tomorrow, it's finished.

ELLIDA (*looking at him, trembling*). Finished?

STRANGER (*nodding*). Finished forever. I'll never come back to Norway. You'll never see me again, or hear from me. So far as you're concerned, I'll be dead and gone.

ELLIDA (*breathing uneasily*). Oh . . .

STRANGER. Think what you're going to do. Think carefully.

He climbs back over the fence, then turns.

That's all, Ellida. Be ready tomorrow evening. That's when I'll fetch you, then.

Exit calmly along the path right. ELLIDA *gazes after him. Pause.*

ELLIDA. Of my own free will. He said I could go, of my own free will.

WANGEL. Don't upset yourself. He's gone. You'll never see him again.

ELLIDA. What d'you mean? He's coming again tomorrow.

WANGEL. He can come if he likes. I'll make sure he doesn't see you.

ELLIDA (*shaking her head*). Don't imagine you'll stop him.

WANGEL. My dear, I can. Just trust me.

ELLIDA (*to herself, ignoring him*). When he's been, tomorrow evening, when he's gone away, in the tour-boat, far across the sea . . .

WANGEL. What then?

ELLIDA. Will he really never come again?

WANGEL. My dear, be sure of it. What point would there be? You told him, plainly, that you'd finished with him. That's the end of it.

ELLIDA (*to herself*). Tomorrow, then. Or never.

WANGEL. And even if he *did* turn up again –

ELLIDA (*eagerly*). What then?

WANGEL. We know how to make him harmless.

ELLIDA. You can't, you can't.

WANGEL. Of course we can. If nothing else will make him leave you alone, I'll see that he's charged with killing that captain.

ELLIDA (*harshly*). You can't. We know nothing about it. The captain's murder – nothing.

WANGEL. Of course we do. He confessed to you.

ELLIDA. No, we know nothing. If you say we do, I'll deny it. Don't put him in prison. His place is the sea, the open sea. He's home there.

WANGEL (*looking at her, slowly*). Oh Ellida, Ellida . . .

ELLIDA (*hugging him*). Oh Edvard, I love you, I trust you, save me from that man.

WANGEL (*gently freeing himself*). Come inside now.

Enter LYNGSTRAND *and* HILDE, *right, round the pond, with their fishing gear.* LYNGSTRAND *hurries to* ELLIDA.

LYNGSTRAND. Mrs Wangel, you'll never guess. It's amazing.

WANGEL. What is?

LYNGSTRAND. We saw the American.

WANGEL. The American?

HILDE. I saw him too.

LYNGSTRAND. He came down the path behind the garden, and boarded that English tour-boat.

WANGEL. You've seen him before?

LYNGSTRAND. I sailed with him once. I thought he'd drowned, but here he is, large as life.

WANGEL. D'you know anything else about him?

LYNGSTRAND. No. Unless he's come to punish the wife who betrayed him.

WANGEL. I beg your pardon?

HILDE. Mr Lyngstrand's making a sculpture of him.

WANGEL. I don't understand a word . . .

ELLIDA. I'll tell you later.

Enter ARNHOLM *and* BOLETTE *left along the path.*

BOLETTE (*over the fence*). Come and look. The boat's just leaving.

A large ship glides slowly past in the distance.

LYNGSTRAND (*to* HILDE, *by the fence*). He'll be back tonight.

HILDE (*nodding*). To punish the wife who betrayed him.

LYNGSTRAND. At the midnight hour.

HILDE. Could be worth watching.

ELLIDA (*looking out after the ship*). Tomorrow, then –

WANGEL. And never afterwards.

ELLIDA (*in a low voice, trembling*). Oh darling, save me from myself.

WANGEL (*with an anxious look*). Ellida . . . this is more than him . . .

ELLIDA. It's the power.

WANGEL. What power?

ELLIDA. That man is like the sea.

Exit slowly through the garden, left, plunged in thought. WANGEL accompanies her, watching her anxiously.

End of Act Three.

ACT FOUR

WANGEL's garden-room. Doors left and right. At rear, between the two windows, an open glass door to the verandah. A good deal of the garden is visible. Down left, sofa and table. Down right, piano, upstage of which is a large flower-stand. In the centre, round table and chairs. On the table, rose bush in flower; other house plants all round.

It is morning. BOLETTE is sitting on the sofa, working on embroidery. LYNGSTRAND is sitting on a dining-chair at the upstage end of the table. His arms are on the table, and he is watching BOLETTE. Out in the garden, BALLESTED is painting, encouraged by HILDE.

LYNGSTRAND (after a pause). Miss Wangel, it must be really difficult to sew edges like that.

BOLETTE. Not really. Not if you count right.

LUNGSTRAND. You have to count?

BOLETTE. The stitches. Look.

LYNGSTRAND. I see what you mean. It's an art-form, almost. D'you know how to draw?

BOLETTE. If I've something to copy.

LYNGSTRAND. Not freehand?

BOLETTE. No.

LYNGSTRAND. So it's not really art.

BOLETTE. More a sort of . . . knack.

LYNGSTRAND. I'm sure you could *learn* to draw.

BOLETTE. I'm really no good at it.

LYNGSTRAND. If you spent your time with a proper artist . . .

BOLETTE. I could learn from him?

LYNGSTRAND. I don't mean 'learn' in the usual way. Gradually, absorb. Miss Wangel, it would be a kind of miracle.

BOLETTE. It certainly would.

Pause.

LYNGSTRAND. Have you ever thought . . . I mean, seriously, properly . . . Miss Wangel, about marriage?

BOLETTE (*giving him a glance*). Ah. No.

LYNGSTRAND. I have.

BOLETTE. Really?

LYNGSTRAND. Oh yes. I think about things like that all the time. Marriage especially. I've studied it in books. In my opinion, marriage itself may be seen as a kind of miracle, in the sense that the wife gradually evolves and changes in her husband's image.

BOLETTE. Takes on his interests?

LYNGSTRAND. Exactly.

BOLETTE. What about his abilities, his talent, his . . . knack?

LYNGSTRAND. Hm. Yes. I don't see why not, given time –

BOLETTE. And also: what he learned by reading, or by contemplation – she could absorb that too?

LYNGSTRAND. Oh yes. Gradually, a kind of miracle. Of course it would only work if the marriage was faithful, loving and utterly happy.

BOLETTE. Have you ever considered that the husband could also evolve? Change, I mean, in *her* image?

LYNGSTRAND. The husband. I don't think so.

BOLETTE. Why not? If it happens the other way?

LYNGSTRAND. A husband has a vision, a calling: that's what makes him strong, makes him steadfast. A vocation, Miss Wangel.

BOLETTE. Every single husband?

LYNGSTRAND. I *was* thinking mainly of artists.

BOLETTE. D'you think an artist *ought* to marry?

LYNGSTRAND. Yes, if he can find someone he really loves.

BOLETTE. I feel an artist should live for his art alone.

LYNGSTRAND. He still can, even if he's married.

BOLETTE. But what about her?

LYNGSTRAND. Who d'you mean?

BOLETTE. The woman he marries. What does *she* live for?

LYNGSTRAND. His art, the same. I'd think any woman would be pleased with that.

BOLETTE. I wonder.

LYNGSTRAND. No, no, Miss Wangel, believe me. It's not just the reflected honour and glory, though that *is* part of it. It's that she can help him to create, ease his path, be always at his side, look after him, make his life agreeable. What woman could ask for anything better?

BOLETTE. Have you any idea how selfish you are?

LYNGSTRAND. Me, selfish? Good Heavens! If you knew me better . . .

He leans forward.

Miss Wangel, once I'm gone – and that may be sooner than you think –

BOLETTE (*with a look of pity*). Oh, don't be so gloomy.

LYNGSTRAND. Why gloomy?

BOLETTE. I don't understand.

LYNGSTRAND. In a month, I start my travels. First, I leave here for home. Then South to the Mediterranean.

BOLETTE. Oh, that's what you meant. Of course.

LYNGSTRAND. Miss Wangel, will you think of me occasionally?

BOLETTE. No doubt of it.

LYNGSTRAND (*delighted*). You promise?

BOLETTE. I promise.

LUNGSTRAND. Cross your heart, Miss Wangel?

BOLETTE. Cross my heart. (*New tone.*) Look, what's the point of all this? Nothing will come of it.

LYNGSTRAND. How can you say so? Don't you think I'll be happy, thinking of you here at home thinking of me?

BOLETTE. Yes, but then what?

LYNGSTRAND. That's as far as I thought.

BOLETTE. There are so many obstacles. The whole world's an obstacle.

LYNGSTRAND. Something might happen . . . a miracle. A lucky chance, who knows? I'm certain luck's on my side.

BOLETTE (*quickly*). Don't ever stop thinking so.

LYNGSTRAND. I'm convinced of it. So then, in a year or two, when I come back again, when I'm a world-famous sculptor, rich, in excellent health –

BOLETTE. So we hope and pray.

LYNGSTRAND. Oh, it'll happen, now you've promised to think of me warmly and faithfully all the time I'm there. In the Mediterranean.

BOLETTE. I promised. (*Shaking her head.*) I still think nothing will come of it.

LYNGSTRAND. Bolette, of course it will. My group, to start with: I'll make enormous progress. It'll be easy.

BOLETTE. You think so?

LYNGSTRAND. I feel it, here. And you'll feel it too – here in the back of beyond – knowing that you're there, in a manner of speaking, helping me, inspiring me . . .

BOLETTE (*looking at him*). And on your side? You?

LYNGSTRAND. Me?

BOLETTE (*looking into the garden*). Sh! Change the subject. Mr Arnholm's coming.

ARNHOLM *has come into the garden, from left, and has stopped to talk to* HILDE *and* BALLESTED.

LYNGSTRAND. Miss Wangel, d'you like your old tutor?

BOLETTE. Like him?

LYNGSTRAND. I mean, are you fond of him?

BOLETTE. Well, naturally. He's a good friend, helpful, full of wise advice . . .

LYNGSTRAND. Isn't it odd he never married?

BOLETTE. Why odd?

LYNGSTRAND. It's not as if he can't afford it.

BOLETTE. I don't imagine so. I think it's just hard for him to find a girl who'll have him.

LYNGSTRAND. Why?

BOLETTE. Every single girl he's met, he's taught. He says so himself.

LYNGSTRAND. What difference does that make?

BOLETTE. For Heaven's sake, girls don't marry their *teachers*!

LYNGSTRAND. Don't they have crushes on them?

BOLETTE. Yes, and then they grow up.

LYNGSTRAND. How extraordinary.

BOLETTE (*warning*). Sh! Sh!

During this, BALLESTED *has gathered his things. He goes off right, through the garden.* HILDE *helps him.* ARNHOLM *comes up the verandah steps and into the room.*

ARNHOLM. My dear, good morning. Good morning, Mr . . . Mr . . . hm . . .

He looks annoyed, and nods frostily to LYNGSTRAND, *who gets up and bows.* BOLETTE *goes to greet him.*

BOLETTE. Mr Arnholm, good morning.

ARNHOLM. How's everyone today?

BOLETTE. Fine, thank you.

ARNHOLM. Has your stepmother gone swimming?

BOLETTE. No, she's upstairs.

ARNHOLM. Not ill, I hope?

BOLETTE. I don't know. She's locked herself in.

ARNHOLM. Good gracious.

LYNGSTRAND. That American yesterday upset her.

ARNHOLM. Excuse me. *You* – ?

LYNGSTRAND. I told her I saw him in the garden.

ARNHOLM. Really.

BOLETTE (*to* ARNHOLM). You and Papa sat up late last night.

ARNHOLM. Important things to settle.

BOLETTE. You mentioned my – ?

ARNHOLM. No, my dear. His mind was on something else.

BOLETTE (*sighing*). It always is.

ARNHOLM *looks hard at her.*

ARNHOLM. But don't forget: you and I are to talk about it, very soon. Where is your father? Has he gone out?

BOLETTE. He'll be at the surgery. I'll fetch him.

ARNHOLM. No, no. I'd prefer to see him there.

BOLETTE (*listening off, left*). Just a minute, he's coming downstairs. He must have been looking after *her.*

Enter WANGEL, *left. He holds out his hand to* ARNHOLM.

WANGEL. My dear chap, you're early. Thanks for coming so soon. We've still a lot to settle.

BOLETTE (*to* LYNGSTRAND). Shall we talk to Hilde in the garden?

LYNGSTRAND. Miss Wangel, nothing would suit me better.

They go into the garden and out through the trees.
ARNHOLM *watches them out of sight, then turns to*
WANGEL.

ARNHOLM. How much do you know about that young man?

WANGEL. Not a lot.

ARNHOLM. You don't mind him spending so much time with the girls?

WANGEL. Does he? I hadn't noticed.

ARNHOLM. I think you should be careful.

WANGEL. Maybe so. But what can I do? They're old enough to look after themselves. They don't listen to me, don't listen to Ellida.

ARNHOLM. I'm surprised.

WANGEL. In any case, I can't ask *her* to . . . It's not *her* (*ie, business*) . . .

He changes the subject.

But that's not what we were supposed to be discussing. Tell me, what I asked you last night: have you thought any more about it?

ARNHOLM. I've thought about nothing else.

WANGEL. What d'you think I ought to do?

ARNHOLM. My dear Wangel, you're the doctor.

WANGEL. Ha. No one realises how hard it is for a doctor to make a good diagnosis when he loves his patient so dearly. And this is no ordinary illness. It needs specialist knowledge, specialist treatment . . .

ARNHOLM. How is she today?

WANGEL. When I was up there just now, she seemed calm enough. But it's as if there's some secret behind all her moods, something I simply can't get at. Her behaviour's erratic . . . unpredictable . . . always changing.

ARNHOLM. Surely that's to be expected, in her mental condition.

WANGEL. It's not just that. It's deeper. Ellida's a sea being. That's what it is.

ARNHOLM. I really don't follow.

WANGEL. Haven't you ever noticed? People who live by the open sea are like separate beings. It's as if they lived the life of the sea itself. Its tides, its surges, its ebb and flow, are there in their hearts, their thoughts. They can't be transplanted. I should have realised before. Taking Ellida from the sea and bringing her here was a crime, a sin.

ARNHOLM. That's how it seems to you?

WANGEL. More and more. I should have known from the start. Oh, I knew it, deep inside, but I ignored it. I loved her so much, and that made me selfish. Utterly, completely – I thought of nothing but myself.

ARNHOLM. In those circumstances, surely all men are a little selfish. Though I can't say I've ever noticed that particular vice in you, Doctor Wangel.

WANGEL (*fidgeting uneasily*). Oh, I was, and I still am. I'm a great deal older than she is. I should have been like a father to her, guide and father. I should have done all I could to draw her out, help her see her way. But I didn't. I didn't *want* to – I preferred her the way she was. And then she began getting worse. I'm at my wits' end. (*Lower.*) That's why I wrote to you, asked you to visit.

ARNHOLM (*staring*). Is *that* why you invited me?

WANGEL. Yes. But don't mention it to anyone.

ARNHOLM. My dear Doctor Wangel, how on earth d'you think *I* can help? I know nothing about these things.

WANGEL. I see that now. I was on a false track. I thought Ellida had been fond of you once, and still was, secretly. I thought it would do her good to see you again, talk to you about the old days, her father's house . . .

ARNHOLM. So when you wrote and said someone was hoping, longing to see me – you meant your wife!

WANGEL. Who else could it have been?

ARNHOLM (*quickly*). No, you're right. I misunderstood, that's all.

WANGEL. As I said before: I was on a wrong track completely.

ARNHOLM. And you call yourself selfish!

WANGEL. After what I'd done, the terrible thing I'd done, I had to atone. I had to try every way I could to help her, to ease her mind.

ARNHOLM. What d'you think it is, the power this stranger has over her?

WANGEL. Um, dear friend . . . there may be a side to this which baffles explanation.

ARNHOLM. You mean something supernatural?

WANGEL. We don't know enough at present –

ARNHOLM. You *believe* in that?

WANGEL. I'm agnostic. No idea. So I suspend my judgement.

ARNHOLM. One thing, tell me: that bizarre idea she has, that fixation, the baby's eyes . . .

WANGEL (*eagerly*). Oh, that's just nonsense. That I *don't* believe. She imagines it, that's all.

ARNHOLM. When that fellow was here yesterday, did you look at his eyes?

WANGEL. Well, of course I did.

ARNHOLM. And was there a likeness?

WANGEL (*evasively*). Hm . . . good lord, I don't know. It was getting dark when I saw him. Ellida has talked so much about the likeness, I don't think I was in any state to make an objective judgement.

ARNHOLM. Maybe not. But the other thing: the fact that all her anxiety and distress began at the exact moment the stranger began coming home?

WANGEL. You see, she must have dreamed *that* as well, persuaded herself. Since the day before yesterday: it wasn't quite as sudden as she claims. As soon as she heard from young Lyngstrand that Johnston, Friman, whatever his name is, set off for home three years ago last March, she convinced herself that her mental problems began at the exact same time.

ARNHOLM. They didn't?

WANGEL. Not remotely. There'd been signs, symptoms, for months. Mind you, by pure coincidence, she did have a bad attack three years ago last March . . .

ARNHOLM. Well then!

WANGEL. But that can be explained by the circumstances, the condition she was in.

ARNHOLM. No proof either way.

WANGEL (*wringing his hands*). To have no way of reaching her, helping her, to see no way out of it –

ARNHOLM. Unless you made up your mind to move, somewhere she might find more like home . . .

WANGEL. My dear man, d'you think I haven't suggested that? I said we should move to Skjoldvik. And she refused.

ARNHOLM. Wouldn't hear of it?

WANGEL. There'd be no point, she says. And perhaps she's right.

ARNHOLM. You agree with her?

WANGEL. In any case, when I think about it properly, I don't see how I could manage it. The girls – I don't see I've the right to drag *them* to the back of beyond. They should live where they stand *some* chance of finding husbands.

ARNHOLM. Husbands already!

WANGEL. What with that, and my poor sick Ellida . . . Oh Arnholm, what am I to do? Fire, water: where am I to turn?

ARNHOLM. At least, so far as Bolette's concerned, you may be able to –

He breaks off.

I wonder where she . . . where they are?

He goes to the window and looks out.

WANGEL. I'd do anything I could, sacrifice anything I could, for the three of them. If only I *knew*!

Enter ELLIDA, left.

ELLIDA (*urgently to* WANGEL). Don't go out this morning.

WANGEL. Don't worry. I'll be home, beside you.

He indicates ARNHOLM, who comes closer.

But you haven't said hello to our friend.

ELLIDA (*turning*). Oh, Mr Arnholm . . .

She holds out her hand.

Good morning.

ARNHOLM. Good morning. No swimming this morning?

ELLIDA. No, no, no. I couldn't, not today. Won't you sit down a moment?

ARNHOLM. Not just now, thanks. (*With a glance at* WANGEL.) I promised the girls I'd join them in the garden.

ELLIDA. Heaven alone knows if you'll find them there. I never know where they are, these days.

WANGEL. They'll be down at the pond.

ARNHOLM. I'll find them.

He nods and exit into the garden, and off right.

ELLIDA. What time is it?

WANGEL (*glancing at his watch*). Just after eleven.

ELLIDA. Just after. And the tour-boat'll be here at half-past eleven or twelve tonight. Oh, if only it was over.

WANGEL (*going closer*). Ellida, darling . . . there's one thing I must ask you.

ELLIDA. What?

WANGEL. Yesterday, at the Viewpoint, you said you'd often seen him these last three years, as if he was there in person.

ELLIDA. I have. It's true, trust me.

WANGEL. What was he like?

ELLIDA. What d'you mean?

WANGEL. I mean, what did he look like when you saw him?

ELLIDA. Edvard, you know what he looks like.

WANGEL. And that's exactly how he looked, each time?

ELLIDA. Yes.

WANGEL. Just like yesterday?

ELLIDA. Exactly the same.

WANGEL. In that case, why didn't you recognise him as soon as you saw him?

ELLIDA (*startled*). Didn't I?

WANGEL. You told me: at first you'd no idea who the stranger was.

ELLIDA (*struck by this*). That's right. Wasn't that odd, I mean not recognising him?

WANGEL. It was his eyes, you said.

ELLIDA. Oh yes. His eyes. His eyes.

WANGEL. But up the Viewpoint you told me that he'd always appeared to you the way he looked when you parted at Bratthammer, ten years ago.

ELLIDA. Did I?

WANGEL. Yes.

ELLIDA. So he must have looked the same then as he does now.

WANGEL. Oh no. You described someone completely different the night before last as we were coming home. Ten years ago he hadn't a beard, you said. Completely different clothes. And the pearl tiepin – the man yesterday had no tiepin.

ELLIDA. That's right, he hadn't.

WANGEL (*looking intently at her*). Ellida, think carefully. Can you remember exactly what he looked like that day at Bratthammer?

ELLIDA (*closing her eyes to think better*). Not exactly. Hardly at all, today. Isn't that peculiar?

WANGEL. You've seen a real person, and it's obliterated the old one, so that you can't see it any more.

ELLIDA. D'you think so, Edvard?

WANGEL. And it blots out your imaginings, too. A dose of reality: best medicine of all.

ELLIDA. What d'you mean?

WANGEL. His coming may be exactly what you needed.

ELLIDA (*sitting on the sofa*). Edvard, sit here a minute. I'll tell you what I think. All of it.

WANGEL. Yes, darling, do.

He sits on a chair facing her across the table.

ELLIDA. It was the worst thing that could happen, for both of us, that we ever met.

WANGEL (*astounded*). What did you say?

ELLIDA. It had to be. It couldn't be anything else. Not the way it happened.

WANGEL. What was wrong with the way it happened?

ELLIDA. Listen to me. It's pointless going on like this, telling lies to ourselves, each other.

WANGEL. What lies?

ELLIDA. We conceal the truth. The plain, blunt truth – that you came out there and . . . bought me.

WANGEL. Bought you?

ELLIDA. I was no better. I went along with it. I sold myself.

WANGEL (*looking at her in anguish*). Ellida, how can you say this?

ELLIDA. What else am I to say? Your house was empty, you couldn't bear it, you looked round for another wife –

WANGEL. A new mother for the children.

ELLIDA. Perhaps, in passing. Though you'd no idea what sort of mother I'd make them. You'd only seen me, spoken to me, a couple of times. You took a fancy to me –

WANGEL. If that's what you call it.

ELLIDA. And on my side: there I was, broken-hearted, alone. You offered to cherish me till the day I died – why shouldn't I say 'yes'?

WANGEL. Ellida, it wasn't *like* that. I never thought of it like that. I asked you, frankly and openly, if you'd share with us, with the children, with me, what little I possessed.

ELLIDA. So you did. But however much it was, or how little, I should have said 'no'. I shouldn't have accepted, at any price. Sold myself. Better poverty, hard labour, of my own free will, my own free choice.

WANGEL (*getting up*). So for you they've been wasted: these last six years, our marriage?

ELLIDA. Don't think that! Here with you – what human being could ask for more? It's just . . . free will, I didn't come to your home of my own free will.

WANGEL (*staring at her*). You mean that?

ELLIDA. Not of my own free will.

WANGEL (*softly*). I remember now: this is what *he* said, yesterday.

ELLIDA. My eyes were opened. I see everything clearly.

WANGEL. What do you see?

ELLIDA. I see that this life we lead, my life with you, your life with me – it's not a marriage.

WANGEL (*bitterly*). Not any more. No marriage.

ELLIDA. And it never was. From the very start. (*Looking straight ahead.*) The first, *that* might have been a marriage.

WANGEL. What d'you mean? What first?

ELLIDA. My first – to him.

WANGEL (*looking at her, amazed*). I don't understand you at all.

ELLIDA. Edvard, let's be honest with each other. And with ourselves.

WANGEL. What d'you mean?

ELLIDA. It's unavoidable. A promise, made with free will, is as binding as a marriage.

WANGEL. For Heaven's sake –

ELLIDA (*jumping up*). Darling, let me leave you.

WANGEL. Ellida! Ellida?

ELLIDA. Let me go. You must. Believe me. There's no alternative. Not after the way we came together.

WANGEL (*crushed, but controlling it*). It's happened.

ELLIDA. It had to happen.

WANGEL (*looking sadly at her*). So not even our life together . . . You've never been mine, entirely mine.

ELLIDA. Oh Edvard, if only I could love you. I want to. But I can't. Not ever.

WANGEL. Divorce, full, formal divorce, is that what you want?

ELLIDA. My dear, you don't understand me, really. Formalities don't matter. The forms of things. I want us to agree, both of us, of our own free will, to let each other go.

WANGEL (*bitterly, nodding slowly*). To cancel the agreement.

ELLIDA (*eagerly*). Exactly.

WANGEL. Ellida, and then what? Have you thought what happens afterwards? To you, to me? What sort of life is left for us?

ELLIDA. Not important. What'll happen will happen. All that matters, all I'm asking for, begging for, is freedom. Set me free again!

WANGEL. Ellida, what you ask . . . this is appalling. Give me time to think about it. Let's talk about it later. And you: you give yourself time to think about . . . what it is you're doing.

ELLIDA. Too late. I have to be free, today!

WANGEL. Why today?

ELLIDA. Because today *he* comes.

WANGEL (*astonished*). The stranger. What's he got to do with it?

ELLIDA. When I meet him, I want to be free, absolutely free.

WANGEL. Free to do what?

ELLIDA. I won't make the excuse that I'm someone else's wife, that the choice isn't mine to make. If I did, any choice I made would be meaningless.

WANGEL. Choice! You talk about choice! In *this*, Ellida: choice!

ELLIDA. It's what I want. Free choice. To send him away, or go with him.

WANGEL. D'you realise what you're saying? Go with him? Put your fate in his hands?

ELLIDA. I put it in your hands. I didn't think twice about it.

WANGEL. But he's a stranger. A total stranger. You know nothing about him.

ELLIDA. I knew even less about you. And still I married you.

WANGEL. You knew the life you were choosing, the kind of life. But this time! You don't know who he is, what he is . . .

ELLIDA (*gazing ahead*). That's the terrible thing.

WANGEL. Absolutely, yes.

ELLIDA. The thing I feel I *must* give way to.

WANGEL (*staring at her*). *Because* it's terrible?

ELLIDA. Yes.

WANGEL (*going nearer*). Ellida, when you call something 'terrible' –

ELLIDA (*thinking it out*). I mean: it terrifies me . . . I long for it.

WANGEL. *Long* for it?

ELLIDA. That most of all.

WANGEL (*slowly*). You *are* from the sea.

ELLIDA. There terror lies.

WANGEL. And in you it lies. *You* terrify . . . you're longed for . . .

ELLIDA. Now you understand.

WANGEL. I've never understood. Never known you at all.

ELLIDA. That's why you must set me free. Free of every tie to you and yours. Now you understand: I'm not who you thought I was. Now we understand, we can separate, of our own free will.

WANGEL (*heavily*). Separate . . . Perhaps it's best . . . Ellida, I can't! For me, what terrifies, what I long for . . . it lies in *you*.

ELLIDA. You mean that.

WANGEL. Let's work to get through today. Calmly, in control, no accidents. I can't – won't – let you go today. For your own sake, Ellida. It's my right, my duty, to protect you.

ELLIDA. Protect against what? Nothing outside is threatening me, has power over me. The terrible thing's inside me, inside my own head, I long for it – what can you do against it?

WANGEL. I can support you, give you strength to fight it.

ELLIDA. If I *choose* to fight it.

WANGEL. You *don't* choose?

ELLIDA. I don't *know!*

WANGEL. Oh Ellida, by tonight it'll all be settled.

ELLIDA (*blurting it out*). Tonight! Settled, forever, settled –

WANGEL. And then tomorrow –

ELLIDA. Tomorrow! Perhaps I'll have thrown away my future, my reality.

WANGEL. Reality?

ELLIDA. A life, an entire, free life, thrown away. For me. And perhaps for him too.

WANGEL (*in a low voice, taking her wrist*). Ellida, do you love this stranger?

ELLIDA. What can I answer? The terror, my terror . . . it lies in him. I feel –

WANGEL. What, feel?

ELLIDA. – that I belong with him.

WANGEL (*lowering his head*). I understand.

ELLIDA. But can you help me, cure me?

WANGEL (*looking sadly at her*). Tomorrow, he'll have sailed. The cloud will be lifted. And then . . . *then* I'll set you free. I promise. We'll cancel the agreement.

ELLIDA. Too late! Tomorrow!

WANGEL (*looking into the garden*). The children. We must think of the children . . .

ARNHOLM, BOLETTE, HILDE *and*
LYNGSTRAND *appear in the garden.* LYNGSTRAND
says goodbye to the others and goes; they come into the house.

ARNHOLM. Well, I have to tell you, we've been making plans.

HILDE. To go out on the fjord this evening and –

BOLETTE. Sh! It's a secret.

WANGEL. Ah, we've been making plans as well.

ARNHOLM. Really?

WANGEL. Tomorrow Ellida's leaving for Skjoldvik for a while.

BOLETTE. Leaving?

ARNHOLM. Mrs Wangel, an excellent idea.

WANGEL. She needs to go home. Home to the sea.

HILDE *runs to* ELLIDA.

HILDE. You're not leaving! Not leaving us!

ELLIDA (*taken aback*). Hilde, what is it?

HILDE (*checking herself*). Nothing. It's all right. (*In a low voice, turning away.*) Go if you want.

BOLETTE (*anxiously*). Papa, this means . . . *you're* going too.

WANGEL. No, no. Now and then, perhaps . . .

BOLETTE. But you'll come back to us?

WANGEL. Naturally.

BOLETTE. Now and then . . .

WANGEL. Now, girls, it's decided.

He walks away from them.

ARNHOLM (*whispering to* BOLETTE). Later, we'll talk.

He goes to talk to WANGEL, *over by the door.*

ELLIDA (*aside to* BOLETTE). What's the matter with Hilde? She seemed quite upset.

BOLETTE. You mean you never noticed? Day after day she . . . she thirsted for . . . and you never noticed?

ELLIDA. Thirsted for what?

BOLETTE. Since the day you came?

ELLIDA. No, what?

BOLETTE. One word of affection from you.

ELLIDA. Ah. So I've work here as well . . .

She puts her hands on her head and gazes ahead, as if hearing conflicting voices and arguments. WANGEL *and* ARNHOLM *come forward, still talking in low voices.* BOLETTE *goes and looks into the side room, right, then opens the door wide.*

BOLETTE. Dinner's served, Papa.

WANGEL (*forcibly controlling himself*). Really, my dear. That's good. Come along, Mr Arnholm. We'll drink a stirrup cup, to the 'lady from the sea'.

Exeunt right.

End of Act Four.

ACT FIVE

The setting is the same as for Act Three. Late evening.
ARNHOLM, BOLETTE, LYNGSTRAND *and* HILDE
are in a boat on the fjord, punting along the shore.

HILDE. Here. We can jump ashore here.

ARNHOLM. No, don't.

LYNGSTRAND. No jumping for me, Miss Wangel.

HILDE. Or you, either, Mr Arnholm?

ARNHOLM. I'd rather not.

BOLETTE. There's the jetty by the bathing-house.

They punt the boat off, right. At the same moment,
BALLESTED *comes along the path right, carrying music and*
a French horn. He waves to them, turns and talks to them. Their
answers come from further and further off.

BALLESTED. Pardon? Yes, the English boat. Its last visit
this year. Don't be long, if you want to hear the music.
(*Shouting.*) Pardon? (*Shaking his head.*) Can't hear you.

Enter ELLIDA *left, her shawl over her head. She is followed*
by WANGEL.

WANGEL. Ellida, wait. There's plenty of time.

ELLIDA. There isn't. He can come any moment.

BALLESTED (*outside, by the garden fence*). Doctor, good evening. Mrs Wangel, good evening.

WANGEL (*peering to make him out*). Who . . . ah, Ballested. There's music this evening?

BALLESTED. The band going through its paces. It's our busy time of year. Tonight it's for the English.

ELLIDA. Is the boat here already?

BALLESTED. Up the fjord, still, at the islands. But it arrives before you know it.

ELLIDA. That's right.

WANGEL (*half to her*). This evening's the last. It won't be here again.

BALLESTED. More's the pity, Doctor Wangel. But that's why we want to turn out in its honour. Yes indeed. You know what the song says, 'Soon happy summer days are done, Ice grips the seaways one by one.'

ELLIDA. Ice in the seaways. What a gloomy thought.

BALLESTED. Yes indeed. For weeks now, months, we've been summer's children, playing in the sun. It'll be hard to get used to the dark again. Well, at first. After all, Mrs Wangel, people *can* accal . . . acclimatise. They can indeed.

He bows and exit left. ELLIDA *gazes out over the fjord.*

ELLIDA. Another half an hour before it's settled. Unbearable.

WANGEL. You're determined to talk to him. In person.

ELLIDA. I have to. I must make my own choice, of my own free will.

WANGEL. Ellida, you *have* no choice. It's impossible. *I* won't have it.

ELLIDA. You can't stop me: not you, not anyone. You can stop me going with him, if that's what I choose, you can keep me here by force. Against my will. That you can do. But my choice is my own, it's inside me, I can choose him, not you – and if that's what I choose, you can't prevent it.

WANGEL. No, I can't.

ELLIDA. There's nothing to help me fight it. Nothing at home to hold me, keep me. No roots in your house. The girls aren't mine, their hearts I mean. They never have been. When I go – *if* I go, tonight with him or tomorrow to Skjoldvik – I've no keys to hand over, no instructions to leave, about anything. No roots in your house. I've never been part of it, at all, from the moment I arrived.

WANGEL. You chose it that way.

ELLIDA. I had no say either way. Things stayed the way they were. I did nothing to change them. Your idea. Yours, no one else's.

WANGEL. I thought it would help you.

ELLIDA. Yes, Edvard. But now there are consequences. Balances, reckonings. There's nothing here to keep me. Nothing in our life together to support me now, help me, nothing . . . I long for.

WANGEL. I accept that, Ellida. And from tomorrow, you'll be free. Free to live your life.

ELLIDA. What you call my life was sidelined the day I married you.

She clasps and unclasps her hands in agitation.

And now, this evening, in half an hour, *he's* coming, the man I rejected, I should have kept faith with as he kept faith with me. He's coming to offer me, for the last and only time, the chance to live my life again, my proper life, it terrifies me, I long for it, I can't let it go. Not of my own free will.

WANGEL. That's why you need a husband, a doctor – to take the burden, decide for you, help you.

ELLIDA. Oh darling, you can't imagine . . . to cling to you, peace, safety, keep them out, the forces that horrify me, I long for them . . . But I can't. No, no, I can't.

WANGEL. Ellida, walk with me a little.

ELLIDA. I can't. I said I'd wait here for him.

WANGEL. There's time.

ELLIDA. D'you think so?

WANGEL. Yes.

ELLIDA. Just a little way, then.

Exeunt down right. At the same moment ARNHOLM and BOLETTE enter upstage by the pond. BOLETTE sees them going.

BOLETTE. Look, there –

ARNHOLM (*low*). Sh. Leave them.

BOLETTE. What's going *on* between them?

ARNHOLM. You've noticed – ?

BOLETTE. What?

ARNHOLM. – anything unusual?

BOLETTE. Dozens of things. Haven't you?

ARNHOLM. The thing is, I –

BOLETTE. You want to be discreet. But you *have* seen something.

ARNHOLM. I think it'll do your stepmother good to get away.

BOLETTE. Do you?

ARNHOLM. If she gets away now and then, it'll do everyone good.

BOLETTE. If she goes to Skjoldvik tomorrow, she won't come back.

ARNHOLM. Whatever makes you think so?

BOLETTE. Wait and see. She won't come back. At least, not while Hilde and I are here.

ARNHOLM. Oh, Hilde –

BOLETTE. Well, perhaps she and Hilde might . . . Hilde's a child still, in her heart of hearts she needs her. With me, it's different. A stepmother, hardly older than I am –

ARNHOLM. Dear Bolette, you may not have long to wait, before you get away.

BOLETTE (*eagerly*). You've spoken to Papa.

ARNHOLM. Yes.

BOLETTE. What did he say?

ARNHOLM. Hm, he was preoccupied, other things on his mind . . .

BOLETTE. I told you.

ARNHOLM. But one thing he did make clear: you mustn't expect him to . . . help you.

BOLETTE. He can't – ?

ARNHOLM. Help, that kind of help, is beyond his means.

BOLETTE (*reproachfully*). You knew that, and you're standing there making fun of me?

ARNHOLM. Of course not. Bolette, dear, this is up to you. No one else. Leaving home or staying: it's up to you.

BOLETTE. Tell me.

ARNHOLM. To go out into the world, study all you want, the things you dream of here at home, thirst for . . . Bolette, live the life you choose, find happiness – it's up to you.

BOLETTE (*clasping her hands*). Oh God . . . It's impossible. If Papa's says he can't . . . if he won't . . . who else in all the world can I turn to?

ARNHOLM. Couldn't you . . . I mean, is it possible you could . . . a helping hand from your old . . . your former tutor?

BOLETTE. Mr Arnholm, you mean *you'd* . . .

ARNHOLM. Support you? Gladly. Words, deeds . . . trust me. What d'you think? Will you . . . accept?

BOLETTE. To see the world, to study . . . I've dreamed of it . . . it seemed impossible . . .

ARNHOLM. It's yours for the asking. All you have to do is choose.

BOLETTE. Choose happiness . . . You'll help me. But how can I . . . accept such a gift, from a stranger?

ARNHOLM. You can accept it from me, Bolette. You can accept anything from me.

BOLETTE (*taking his hands*). I don't know what it is . . . (*Blurting out.*) I don't know whether I'm crying or laughing. I'm so happy. To live . . . I was afraid the chance would never . . .

ARNHOLM. Bolette, there's nothing to be afraid of. Tell me, bluntly: is there anything, any tie that keeps you here?

BOLETTE. Keeps me? No.

ARNHOLM. Truly?

BOLETTE. I mean . . . Papa's a tie, if that's what you mean. And Hilde. But . . .

ARNHOLM. Look: one day or another, you'd be leaving your father anyway. And Hilde will be making her own way in life, soon, it's a matter of time that's all. I mean, nothing else, Bolette? No *other* ties?

BOLETTE. No, none. I'm a free agent, I can go anywhere I like.

ARNHOLM. In that case, my dear, you can come away with me.

BOLETTE (*clapping her hands*). It's wonderful.

ARNHOLM. You . . . do have faith in me?

BOLETTE. Entirely.

ARNHOLM. You'd be happy to put yourself in my hands – yourself, your future? That would be all right?

BOLETTE. Of course it would. My old tutor . . . I mean, my tutor years ago.

ARNHOLM. Not just that. That's not important. It's . . . I mean, Bolette, now you're free . . . no ties to hold you back . . . would you . . . I wonder . . . would you agree to unite with me . . . for life?

BOLETTE (*startled*). What are you asking?

ARNHOLM. Bolette, I'm asking you to marry me.

BOLETTE (*half to herself*). No, no, no. Not happening. Impossible.

ARNHOLM. You say it's impossible –

BOLETTE. Mr Arnholm, you don't mean what you're saying. You . . .

She looks at him.

Was *this* what you meant when you offered to do so much for me?

ARNHOLM. Bolette, it seems I've . . . taken you by surprise.

BOLETTE. From you, of all people – a proposal. Of course I'm surprised.

ARNHOLM. You'd no idea – how could you have? – that it was because of *you* I came here in the first place?

BOLETTE. Because of me?

ARNHOLM. Your father wrote to me last spring. Something in the letter, a phrase in the letter, made me think . . . mm . . . that your feelings for your former tutor were . . . more than just friendly.

BOLETTE. Papa wrote that?

ARNHOLM. It seems that wasn't what he meant at all. But in the meantime I'd got used to the idea that there was a girl, a young woman, waiting, longing for me to come back. No, darling, don't say anything. The thing is, when a man . . . like me . . . when a man's not . . . as young as he was . . . ideas like that, right or wrong, take hold, firm hold. My feelings for you . . . gratitude, affection . . . grew stronger and stronger. I felt I had to come, had to see you again, tell you I shared the feelings I thought you felt for me.

BOLETTE. But now, when you know it wasn't . . . it was a misunderstanding . . .

ARNHOLM. Doesn't change things. Bolette, whenever I think of you, my thoughts will be always coloured by the feelings that misunderstanding awoke in me. You may find it hard to believe. But it's true.

BOLETTE. If I'd ever thought such a thing was possible . . .

ARNHOLM. It is. You see it is. Oh Bolette, can't you . . . won't you . . . ? Please say you'll marry me.

BOLETTE. But you were my *tutor*. I've never . . . I can't . . . how can I think of you any other way?

ARNHOLM. If you can't, you can't. Never mind. My dear, the rest of our arrangement stands unaltered.

BOLETTE. Pardon?

ARNHOLM. Naturally I'll do what I promised. I'll see that you get away from here, study, whatever you want, find independence, happiness. I'll provide for you, Bolette: I'll always be a friend you can trust, depend on absolutely. Never doubt me.

BOLETTE. Mr Arnholm – don't you understand? – this is out of the question.

ARNHOLM. I don't see why.

BOLETTE. After what you've told me . . . after the answer I gave you . . . to accept such a favour . . . to accept anything now . . . I can't.

ARNHOLM. You'd rather stay here forever, watch life pass by?

BOLETTE. Unbearable.

ARNHOLM. You'll give up all hope of seeing the outside world, of doing all the things you thirst for? Your words. To have so many ambitions, possibilities – and see none of them? Bolette, how can you?

BOLETTE. You're right.

ARNHOLM. And then, when your father's . . . when he . . . you'll be alone, no one to look after you. Or you'll marry someone else, someone you . . . may not even care for, any more than you care for me.

BOLETTE. It's true. All you say is true. But I . . . Or maybe –

ARNHOLM (*quickly*). Maybe?

BOLETTE (*looks undecided at him*). Maybe, after all, it's not impossible.

ARNHOLM. Bolette, what isn't?

BOLETTE. For me to . . . perhaps . . . agree . . . to what you suggest.

ARNHOLM. You mean, you'll let me help you, give me the joy of being a dear and loyal friend?

BOLETTE. That's not what I meant. Not now. Mr Arnholm . . . if you'll have me . . .

ARNHOLM. Bolette –

BOLETTE. I think I . . . I accept.

ARNHOLM. You'll marry me?

BOLETTE. If you'll have me.

ARNHOLM. If I'll . . .

He takes her hand.

Thank you, Bolette, thank you. What you said before . . . when you hesitated . . . it doesn't deter me. You may not care for me now, but you will, I'll win your heart. Oh Bolette, take such care of you.

BOLETTE. I'm to travel, see the world, see life. You promised.

ARNHOLM. I'll keep my promise.

BOLETTE. Study anything I want to.

ARNHOLM. I'll help you, show you, just as before. D'you remember the last year I was your tutor . . . ?

BOLETTE (*quietly, absorbed in her thoughts*). Freedom. The unknown. Escape. No fears for the future, no worries over money . . .

ARNHOLM. Never, Bolette, nevermore. That's something, too. Bolette . . .

BOLETTE. No doubt of it.

ARNHOLM (*putting his arm round her waist*). We'll be so comfortable, so easy. We'll get on so well . . . such peace, such trust . . .

BOLETTE. Yes. I think we will.

She looks off right, and quickly breaks free.

Don't say a word about it.

ARNHOLM. My dear, what's the matter?

BOLETTE. That poor . . . (*pointing*) Over there.

ARNHOLM. Your father?

BOLETTE. The sculptor. He's walking with Hilde.

ARNHOLM. Oh, Lyngstrand. Why should he upset you?

BOLETTE. You know how frail he is, how sick.

ARNHOLM. How he thinks he is.

BOLETTE. No, it's real. He hasn't long. And perhaps it's as well.

ARNHOLM. What d'you mean?

BOLETTE. Well, his . . . it won't amount to anything. His art. Let's go before they come.

ARNHOLM. My dear, if you say so.

HILDE *and* LYNGSTRAND *come round the pond.*

HILDE. Hey. Wait. What's the matter? Wait.

ARNHOLM. Bolette and I . . . we'd like to . . . we . . .

He and BOLETTE *go out left.*

LYNGSTRAND (*chuckling*). It's something in the air. Everyone goes around in pairs. One pair, another pair, always in pairs.

HILDE (*looking after them*). I think he's sweet on her.

LYNGSTRAND. Really?

HILDE. It's obvious, if you know what to look for.

LYNGSTRAND. Bolette won't have him. I'm telling you.

HILDE. She thinks he's too old. Not to mention bald.

LYNGSTRAND. No, something else. She wouldn't have him anyway.

HILDE. How d'you know?

LYNGSTRAND. There's someone else. She promised to keep him in her thoughts.

HILDE. In her thoughts?

LYNGSTRAND. While he was away.

HILDE. You, you mean.

LYNGSTRAND. It could be.

HILDE. She promised?

LYNGSTRAND. Yes. But please don't tell her I told you.

HILDE. Don't worry. My lips are sealed.

LYNGSTRAND. It was really nice of her.

HILDE. And when you come back, there'll be an engagement? You'll marry her?

LYNGSTRAND. Good Heavens, no. For the first few years, I've my career to think of, not marriage. And by the time I'm famous, she'll be past it, well past it.

HILDE. But she's to keep you in her thoughts?

LYNGSTRAND. It's important. For my work. And it's not as if it's difficult: she's nothing else to aspire to. But still, it's nice of her.

HILDE. You think you'll do better work – that group of yours – if Bolette keeps you in her thoughts?

LYNGSTRAND. Well, obviously. To know that somewhere in the world a young, pretty, silent woman is sitting dreaming of me . . . well, it must be . . . I mean, it'll be . . . I can't think of the word.

HILDE. Exciting?

LYNGSTRAND. That's it. Exciting. That's what I mean.

He looks at her a moment.

You're bright, you know. Really bright. When I come back again, you'll be the same age then as your sister is now. Perhaps you'll be as pretty . . . perhaps your character will have grown more like hers. I mean, perhaps you'll be, if you see what I mean, her and you, both, in the same body, a kind of . . . *gestalt.*

HILDE. You'd like that?

LYNGSTRAND. D'you know, I don't know. Yes, I think so. But now, this summer, I want you to be just yourself. No one else. Just the way you are.

HILDE. You *want* me like this?

LYNGSTRAND. Very much indeed.

HILDE. Hm. Tell me. You're an artist. These light summer dresses I wear: d'you think they suit me?

LYNGSTRAND. Oh yes.

HILDE. Summer colours?

LYNGSTRAND. Perfect.

HILDE. Tell me. You're an artist. What would it be like if I dressed in black?

LYNGSTRAND. Black, Miss Wangel?

HILDE. Head to foot in black. D'you think it'd suit me?

LYNGSTRAND. I don't think black, in summer . . . No, I think it *would*. After all, you've got the figure.

HILDE (*gazing ahead*). Black up to here . . . black edging . . . black gloves . . . a long black veil . . .

LYNGSTRAND. Miss Hilde, if you dressed like that, I'd wish I was a painter. A portrait: the young, beautiful, grieving widow.

HILDE. A young bride, cruelly widowed.

LYNGSTRAND. But surely you don't *want* to dress in black?

HILDE. It's exciting.

LYNGSTRAND. Exciting?

HILDE. Exciting to think about. (*Pointing off left.*) Look. Over there.

LYNGSTRAND (*looking*). The English tour-boat. Putting in to the pier.

WANGEL *and* ELLIDA *come in round the pond.*

WANGEL. You're wrong, Ellida. I'm telling you. (*Seeing the others.*) Ah, you two. Mr Lyngstrand, she's not in yet?

LYNGSTRAND. The English tour-boat?

WANGEL. Yes.

LYNGSTRAND (*pointing*). See for yourself, Doctor.

ELLIDA. I knew it was.

WANGEL. It's here.

LYNGSTRAND. Like a thief in the night, to coin a phrase. Stealthily, silently . . .

WANGEL. Take Hilde down to the pier. Please. Hurry. She'll enjoy the music.

LYNGSTRAND. We were just on our way.

WANGEL. We'll follow you later. Probably.

HILDE (*aside to* LYNGSTRAND). Yet another couple.

She and LYNGSTRAND *go out through the garden, left. From the fjord in the distance, a band can be heard. The music continues under the following scene.*

ELLIDA. He's come. He's here. I feel it.

WANGEL. Ellida, you go in. Leave me to deal with him.

ELLIDA. Impossible. Impossible. (*With a sudden shriek.*) Look there. He's coming.

The STRANGER *comes in left down the path and stops outside the garden gate. He bows.*

STRANGER. Ellida, good evening. I said I'd come.

ELLIDA. Yes, yes, it's now.

STRANGER. Are you ready? Are you coming or not?

WANGEL. You can see she isn't.

STRANGER. I don't mean travelling-clothes, luggage. All she needs is on board already. Her cabin – seen to. (*To* ELLIDA.) I'm asking you, are you ready to come with me, of your own free will?

ELLIDA (*imploring*). Don't ask me. Don't tempt me.

The ship's bell is heard, off.

STRANGER. The warning bell. Yes or no: you have to choose.

ELLIDA (*wringing her hands*). One choice. My whole life, one choice. No second chance.

STRANGER. In half an hour, it'll be too late.

ELLIDA (*gazing fearfully at him*). Why do you cling so stubbornly?

STRANGER. We belong to each other. I feel it. Don't you feel it?

ELLIDA. Because we promised?

STRANGER. Promises bind no one. Neither men nor women. I cling so stubbornly because . . . I've no other choice.

ELLIDA (*low, trembling*). Why didn't you come sooner?

WANGEL. Ellida.

ELLIDA (*blurting it*). Into the unknown, it's dragging me, tempting, calling . . . The sea, the strength of it, all here . . .

The STRANGER *climbs over the fence. She cowers behind* WANGEL.

What d'you want of me? What d'you want of me?

STRANGER. Ellida, I see it, hear it. Inside you. It's me you choose.

WANGEL (*advancing on him*). The choice isn't hers. I'm choosing for her, protecting her. Protecting her. Unless you clear off, now, leave the country, you know what to expect.

ELLIDA. Edvard, don't.

STRANGER. What will you do to me?

WANGEL. I'll have you arrested – for murder. Before you get back on board. I know all about Skjoldvik, the murder at Skjoldvik.

ELLIDA. Edvard. How can you – ?

STRANGER. I thought this might happen.

He takes a pistol from his breast pocket. ELLIDA *throws herself in front of* WANGEL.

ELLIDA. No, no. Shoot me, not him.

STRANGER. Neither of you. Don't worry. This is for me. I'll live and die a free man.

ELLIDA (*more and more distraught*). Edvard, let me say one thing. Let him hear me say it. You can keep me here. You can, no one can stop you. And you will. But my mind, my thoughts, my longings, the desires that tug me – you can't stop them. They'll push and strain, out into the unknown, the unknown I was born for, the unknown you've barred me from.

WANGEL (*quietly and sadly*). Ellida, step by step, you're slipping away from me. All that's boundless, limitless, untouchable – you reach for it, crave it, it'll push you into the dark, over the brink into the endless dark . . .

ELLIDA. Wings, beating, hovering, dark wings beating . . .

WANGEL. All right. There's no other way to save you. None I can see, at any rate. So: I break our agreement. It's over. Go where you please, in full free will.

ELLIDA *stares as if speechless. Then*:

ELLIDA. D'you mean it? It's true? You really mean it?

WANGEL. I mean it. I've nothing. I mean it.

ELLIDA. How can you bring yourself – ?

WANGEL. For you. My love for you.

ELLIDA (*low, trembling*). I mean so much to you?

WANGEL. Over the years . . . you mean so much.

ELLIDA (*clasping her hands*). I never noticed.

WANGEL. Your mind was somewhere else. But now you're free, of me and everything to do with me. Your own proper life: it's yours. You're free to choose: your full responsibility, your choice.

ELLIDA *grips her head with her hands and stares at him.*

ELLIDA. Responsibility. My choice. This is . . . something new.

The ship's bell rings, off.

STRANGER. Ellida. The bell. Come, now.

ELLIDA *looks him in the eye and says, with determination*:

ELLIDA. Not after this.

STRANGER. You're staying?

ELLIDA (*clinging to* WANGEL). After this, how can I leave you?

WANGEL. Ellida. Ellida.

STRANGER. It's finished?

ELLIDA. Finished forever.

STRANGER. There's something here, stronger than all my will.

ELLIDA. For me, your will's a feather. For me, you're dead – a corpse. You came home from the sea, and now you're going back. You terrified me, I longed for you – no more.

STRANGER. Mrs Wangel, goodbye.

He vaults the fence.

From this moment, for me, you cease to exist. A ship-wreck. You're in my past.

Exit left. Pause. WANGEL *looks at* ELLIDA.

WANGEL. Ellida, your mind is like the sea. It ebbs and flows. Why did you change?

ELLIDA. I changed . . . don't you understand? From the moment I had free will, I had to change.

WANGEL. The unknown – d'you long for it still?

ELLIDEA. Neither long for it nor fear it. I could have gone there, seen it, become part of it. I had that choice, free choice, and I chose to reject it.

WANGEL. You think in pictures, pictures in the imagination. Your longing for the sea, yearning for it, the way you were drawn to that stranger – it was freedom you needed, nothing else: to be set free. Free.

ELLIDA. I don't know what to answer. You cured me. You found the right cure, and you were brave enough to use it. No one else could help me.

WANGEL. When the case is desperate, a doctor's brave. Ellida, you'll stay with me?

ELLIDA. Edvard, my dear, I will. I can. In freedom, of my own free will, my full responsibility, my choice.

WANGEL (*gazing affectionately at her*). Ellida. Ellida. One life, united –

ELLIDA. Our memories, mine and yours, united.

WANGEL. Oh darling.

ELLIDA. Our children –

WANGEL. Ours, you call them?

ELLIDA. I'll make them mine.

WANGEL. Our children . . .

He kisses her hands, quickly, joyfully.

Thank you, oh thank you . . .

Enter HILDE, BALLESTED, LYNGSTRAND,
ARNHOLM *and* BOLETTE, *left. They come into the
garden. Groups of young people and tourists stroll along the path.*

HILDE (*aside to* LYNGSTRAND). Don't they look *engaged*,
the pair of them?

BALLESTED (*who has overheard*). It *is* still summer, missie.

ARNHOLM (*looking at* WANGEL *and* ELLIDA). The
tour-boat's sailed.

BOLETTE (*at the fence*). You can see it best from here.

LYNGSTRAND. Last trip this year.

BALLESTED. 'Ice grips the seaways', as the poem says.
Heigho, Mrs Wangel! I hear that you're leaving us too,
for a while. Off to Skjoldvik tomorrow . . .

WANGEL. No. Change of plans. This evening we've
changed our plans.

ARNHOLM (*looking at them*). You have.

BOLETTE (*coming forward*). It's true, Papa?

HILDE (*going to* ELLIDA). You're staying?

ELLIDA. Yes, if you want me.

HILDE (*struggling between tears and joy*). If I . . . oh, if I . . .

ARNHOLM (*to her*). This is a real surprise!

ELLIDA (*smiling gravely*). The thing is, Mr Arnholm . . .

D'you remember what we were saying yesterday? You become a land animal . . . you never go back to the sea. The old sea-life. You never go back.

BALLESTED. Just what happened to my mermaid.

ELLIDA. Very similar.

BALLESTED. Except that the mermaid *dies*. Humans, on the other hand, they can aj . . . can accal . . . accal . . . acclimatise themselves. That's it, Mrs Wangel, acclimatise.

ELLIDA. Free will, Mr Ballested. Free choice.

WANGEL. Full responsibility.

ELLIDA (*quickly, holding out her hand to him*). That's how it is.

The tour-boat passes slowly down the fjord. We hear music from it, close inshore.

End of the Play.

Prounciation of Proper Names

WANGEL (VANG-el)
ELLIDA (el-EE-da)
BOLETTE (bo-LET-teh)
HILDE (HEEL-deh)
ARNHOLM (ARN-holm: NB 'o' as in 'hot' and pronounce
   the 'l' – not 'home')
LYNGSTRAND (LEENG-stran)
BALLESTED (ball-es-STED)
SKIVE (SHEE-veh)
JENSEN (YEN-s'n)
SKJOLDVIK (SHOL-veek)
FRIMAN (FREE-man)

Other names and places as they look.